# Denver Botanic Gardens

## GARDENING WITH ALTITUDE:
### *Cultivating a New Western Style*

*Lewisia cotyledon*

# Denver Botanic Gardens

## Gardening with Altitude:
### Cultivating a New Western Style

**Photography**:
Scott Dressel-Martin

**Published by**:
Denver Botanic Gardens

Text copyright © 2006 Denver Botanic Gardens

All photographs copyright ©2006 Scott Dressel-Martin
unless specifically credited next to photograph.

All rights reserved. No part of this book may be reproduced, stored in a retrieval system, or transmitted in any form or by any means, electronic, mechanical, photocopying, recording, or otherwise, without written permission from the publisher.

Editor:
Holly Shrewsbury

Project Manager:
Deb Golanty

Authors:
Panayoti Kelaidis
Dan Johnson
Mark Fusco
Joe Tomocik
Nick Snakenberg
Margaret Foderaro
Dr. Anna Sher
Thomas Grant

Plant Name Editors:
Cindy Tejral
Ann Berthe

Design:
Jeffrey W. Kinney

Published in 2006 by
Denver Botanic Gardens
1005 York Street
Denver, Colorado 80206, U.S.A.
(720) 865-3500
www.botanicgardens.org

Editorial services by Alice Levine, Boulder, Colorado.
Printed by Johnson Press, Boulder, Colorado.

---

ISBN 10: 0-9777375-0-0
ISBN 13: 978-0-9777375-0-5
0 9 8 7 6 5 4 3 2 1

Library of Congress Control Number:
2006922900

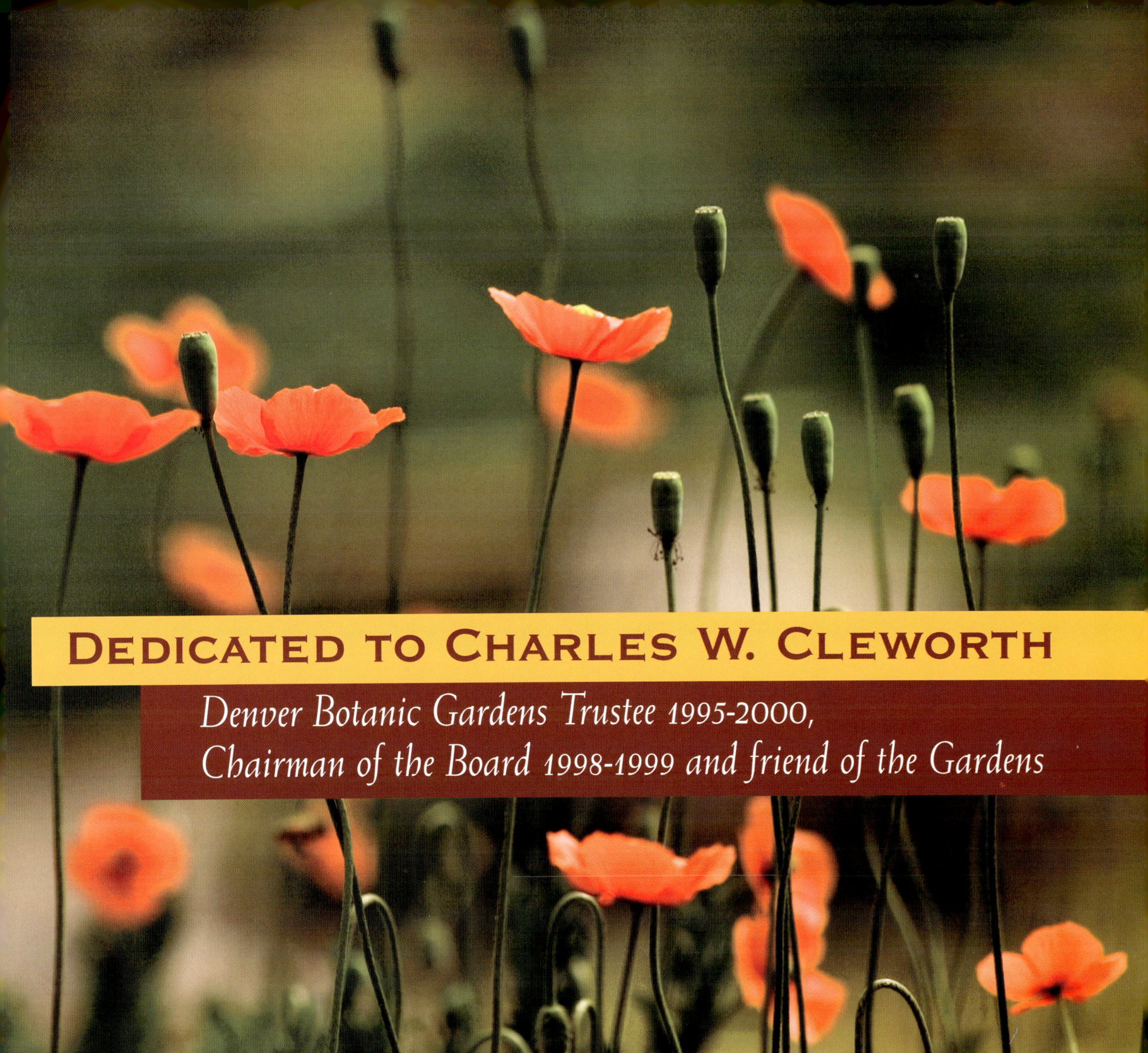

# TABLE OF CONTENTS

Introduction ............................................. 1
Chapter 1   Creating a Sense of Place ................... 4
Chapter 2   Going Native in the Gardens .............. 26
Chapter 3   Tale of the Tundra ....................... 48
Chapter 4   The Allure of Water ...................... 70
Chapter 5   The Gardens Under Glass ................. 92
Chapter 6   Versailles on the Platte ................ 114
Chapter 7   The Public Garden as Science ........... 136

Appendices
Appendix I: About the Authors .......... 148-149
Appendix II: Bibliography ................. 150-151
Appendix III: Index .......................... 152-162
Appendix IV: Order Form ................. 167

# PREFACE

For more than 50 years, Denver Botanic Gardens (referred to affectionately as "the Gardens") has been recognized as a source of inspiration for gardeners throughout the world. Now, for the first time, the Gardens' own horticulture and conservation staff share their expertise, design insights and plant know-how in this beautiful, enlightening book. If you've ever asked yourself, "why can't I grow what I used to grow 'back home'?," "why can't I plant the same plant and have it look like it does at the Gardens?", or "what *can* I grow in this climate?" – this book is for you.

The authors tell the behind-the-scenes story of this institution's signature gardens, whose breathtaking design, plant selection from the far corners of the world and painstaking care represent a fusion of artistry and plant science that sets a new western standard. Located on 23 acres in the center of the Mile High City, Denver Botanic Gardens was one of the first botanic gardens in the United States to showcase native plants of the Great Plains, Rocky Mountain and inter-mountain regions. The Gardens champions environmentally responsible practices, such as Water-Smart Gardening® and conservation biology. Today, Denver Botanic Gardens expands upon this commitment at three additional sites – Denver Botanic Gardens at Chatfield, Centennial Gardens and Mount Goliath – where visitors can experience the varied ecosystems of Colorado, all of which are portrayed in this book.

There have been some horticulturists who have written about their experience in this region, but this is the first time that a collective group of experienced horticulturists have come together to share their knowledge. As a result, this book contains not only techniques but ways of thinking about how your own garden can be in harmony with nature in a semi-arid, high-altitude environment – celebrating, not fighting, this region's climate and growing conditions.

The Gardens is a labor of love and life for the hundreds of thousands of members, volunteers and visitors who come to its four locations. It represent a window to nature, four-season locales where people come to reassess their sense of place, and to confirm their innate connection to the plant world.

This book draws on the finest work of Denver Botanic Gardens' horticulturists and conservation specialists – including Panayoti Kelaidis, Dan Johnson, Mark Fusco, Joe Tomocik, Nick Snakenberg, Margaret Foderaro, Tom Grant and Dr. Anna Sher. Their personal perspectives will engage your imagination. The lavish photography of Scott Dressel-Martin will help you envision plants in new ways, so that you will watch nature unfolding and changing right before your eyes every day.

A dynamic copy, photography and design team helped shape the book's spirit and style – including designer Jeffrey Kinney. Their passion, zest, teamwork and dedication to the Gardens helped make this book come to fruition.

Special thanks go out to all of the staff, volunteers, Board of Trustees and friends of Denver Botanic Gardens – their enthusiasm and stewardship is what keeps the spirit of the institution thriving. The Scientific and Cultural Facilities District (SCFD), which is a special regional tax district that distributes more than $35 million to cultural institutions throughout the Denver metro area, truly helps the Gardens continue to exert great influence not just locally, but on an international level…and for that, we are forever grateful.

Holly Shrewsbury, Editor
Public Relations Manager
Denver Botanic Gardens

# Foreword

Botanic gardens in North America come in many forms and styles. Historically, the purpose of most botanic gardens was to grow the new plants making their way into America with special emphasis on agricultural crops and plants that were useful for medicine and economy. Initially, crops grown in botanic gardens were introduced by European and Spanish settlers. As collections expanded, gardens began to work on taxonomic studies that were initiated with plants from around the world. Interest began to focus on the exotic plants that were being collected in far corners of the world, often creating a sensation among plant enthusiasts; the more rare and unusual, the better. But times have changed, and botanic gardens are emphasizing the recognition and understanding of their regional uniqueness. Plant conservation and sustainability have developed as priorities for many botanic gardens through their education and research programs.

From the start, Denver Botanic Gardens has been a distinctive example of gardening possibilities in the semi-arid West. While understanding the sensitivities of the High Plains climate, the Gardens has played a pivotal role in demonstrating and showcasing horticultural practices as well as growing a huge range of plants that will happily thrive in the semi-arid climate. Many visitors have had eye-opening experiences, discovering the enormous palette of plant choices that will thrive in what was once considered an inhospitable gardening environment.

The Gardens has evolved as one of the national leaders for horticulture in the West. Its vast plant collections range from an extraordinary collection of beautifully displayed alpine plants, roses, herbs, tropicals, perennials, trees and plants appropriate for a Japanese garden, to native and naturalized plants that require less water and thrive in the region. Through its educational programs, the Gardens has inspired visitors to happily engage in Rocky Mountain water-wise gardening, which has encouraged and influenced a gardening renaissance throughout the Denver area and beyond.

By creating a series of styles through innovative garden designs, the Gardens has been able to show creative ways to use plants in a variety of landscapes. Utilizing the talents of local and national landscape architects and designers, their thematic gardens present original and regionally appropriate designs to serve as examples for homeowners. There are opportunities to study and learn from a range of creatively coordinated styles; some are formal in their approach while others take the opposite naturalistic style.

Ornamental plant display and evaluation is ongoing. The Gardens has taken the lead in its evaluation and plant introduction program of superior plants with appeal to the nursery trade and the general public. As the Gardens continues its development, it is a champion of sustainable practices, such as water conservation, and demonstrates the varied and extraordinary ecosystems of Colorado.

Through its broad variety of gardens, programs, plants and activities, the Gardens continues to inspire a new and appropriate approach for gardeners in the West. Led by the talented staff and authors of this book, Rocky Mountain horticulture is being demonstrated with exciting ideas and possibilities for this century and beyond.

Holly H. Shimizu
Executive Director
United States Botanic Garden
Washington, D.C.

*Iris lactea*

# INTRODUCTION

The early settlers and homesteaders who moved into the Denver region in the 1870s were certainly a hardy bunch. They faced a real horticultural trauma head-on when they settled into this semi-arid climate, with annual precipitation of only 14-17 inches a year. I admire their tenacity while trekking over the prairies.

Included in their emigrant bundles, loaded onto wagons were Harison and Austrian copper roses, along with fruit tree slips to plant in this very unforgiving climate. In small ghost towns throughout eastern Colorado, you often encounter the sad remnants of fruit trees scattered about the ruins of an abandoned homestead. The key to growing these plants and trees was water, and without it survival was not possible. As recently as 1971, the Arapahoe County (Colorado) Soil Survey opined that only long or short grasses could grow here, with some scattered willows and cottonwoods in the washes, or some pines on rocky outcroppings. (How water diversions have expanded those options!)

One of the earliest horticulturists to change the notion that Colorado's Front Range was suitable only for the growth of grasses was George W. Kelly, who was the first editor for *The Green Thumb*, the old membership newsletter of Denver Botanic Gardens. His now classic book *Rocky Mountain Horticulture*, first published in 1958, was *the* guide for gardeners in Colorado until the writing of this updated compendium for "what grows here." George wrote several other paperbound guides, such as *Trees* (1976), *Shrubs* (1979), *Flowers* (1981) and *Groundcovers of the Rocky Mountains* (1985), which were all based on research on what was able to grow in Colorado. His sidekick, and onetime partner, was the wonderfully gregarious Harry Swift, whose nursery on the northwest side of town stocked all sorts of new varieties suitable for growing in our beautiful but often adverse-for-plants climate.

Portait of George W. Kelly
(Artist Olga J. Miniclier)

Other pioneers in Rocky Mountain horticulture taught us to vary our plant selection rather than mimic eastern U.S. prototypes. They included Al Rollinger, who made new plant introductions, and Paul Maslin, who truly introduced us to the Rocky Mountain rock garden and its multitudinous varieties of plant selection. Maslin's protégé, Panayoti Kelaidis (who contributed mightily to this book), is the current "Pied Piper" of plant lovers. He has traveled much of the world looking at and studying ecosystems similar to our own and introducing plants that can suitably color our gardens. Among his other honors, Panayoti is a Member-at-Large of the Garden Club of America. He and his plant-curious wife, Gwen, have grown a wonderful Denver garden of experimental plants to prove their point. Panayoti's encyclopedic knowledge has been sought by all manner of plantsmen in the region. This has lead to the introduction of the Plant Select® program, co-sponsored by Colorado State University, Denver Botanic Gardens, horticulturists and nurseries to help gardeners in the Rocky Mountain West plant and grow appropriately.

# Introduction

Now nearly 50 years later, this book presents an amazing update of George Kelly's initial gallant effort. Obviously water is often the key, but as has been found and written about by Dan Johnson in Chapter 2, many showy and unique plants can be grown in Colorado's Front Range that few would have imagined planting before. These require little, if any, water after planting. Denver Botanic Gardens' primary objective, beyond creating a beautiful garden, is to educate gardeners and amateur horticulturists to what might be appropriately (and inappropriately in some cases) grown in this region. Many proficient horticulturists on staff at Denver Botanic Gardens have contributed greatly from their specialties in the writing of this book. It is a privilege to have such a dedicated and friendly staff that is eager to help us learn and apply from the lessons they have learned.

The index to this book shows the wide variety of choices that are now available to us gardeners, and we must thank the Gardens' horticulturists for their efforts. Native gardens, alpine gardens, water gardens, tropical gardens under glass, formal gardens – all are investigated and explained in this book by some talented and imaginative horticulturists of the Gardens. It is an update that has been long needed and awaited. An amazing variety of plant life has been introduced at the Gardens in the last 20 years by Panayoti Kelaidis, Dan Johnson, Mark Fusco, Joe Tomocik, Nick Snakenberg and Margaret Foderaro – all contributors to this valuable book.

In addition, plant researchers and conservationists Anna Sher and Tom Grant introduce us to the invasive plants that have voraciously taken over the plains, gardens and waterways of the West. Herculean efforts will have to be made to control and/or eradicate these intruders. Who would have thought that the starling, sparrow, mongoose, kudzu vine, tamarisk, Russian olive or thistle and numerous others might be inappropriate introductions to our landscape? The last chapter in this book blows a necessary clarion call for us to be on our guard.

On a personal note I must confess that when I first arrived in Denver in the early 1960s, I planted my new garden on the plains with my favorite Midwestern varieties and wondered why they didn't spring into life. I sold that house and left my pitiful initial attempts to the new owner! What a joy it was to learn of George Kelly and absorb my new textbook of plants appropriate to my new ecosystem on my new property. Now we have the next and newest generation of horticulturists imparting their vast knowledge to us. I have already altered my garden. I know you will enjoy this much needed book as much as I have.

Edward P. Connors – Life Trustee, Denver Botanic Gardens
Member-at-Large, Garden Club of America

Foxtail cactus (*Coryphantha missouriensis*)

# CREATING A SENSE OF PLACE

By Panayoti Kelaidis

Who doesn't yearn from time to time for a contemplative place where nature and one's soul are in harmony?

There seems to be a secret garden in everyone's past. Many of us can trace our passion for gardens to an epiphany: Often under lightly overcast skies, vibrant flowers, idyllic vistas, mossy paths, multi-hued butterflies and fragrant scents combine just so to galvanize the acute sensitivity of a child. Who doesn't yearn from time to time for a contemplative place where nature and one's soul are in harmony? Each secret garden is sculpted in our mind's eye from books we have read, photographs we have seen, and places we have visited.

Many of us who love gardens visit and admire some of the thousands of public and private gardens in the United States, Canada, Europe and Asia. The overwhelming majority of these are situated either in moist or perhaps Mediterranean climate regions where gardening has been pursued for centuries, if not millennia. There are more than 1,000 public gardens in Britain alone, for example, and all are fabulous; but they (like others in similar climates) are often repetitive. When we come home, we soon realize that those gardens (and the secret ones in our mind's eye) are difficult—if not impossible—to replicate in Colorado.

Mile High Border with yarrow (*Achillea* 'Moonshine') in foreground and torch lily (*Kniphofia* 'Shining Sceptre') behind.

CREATING A SENSE OF PLACE

Sacred Earth in autumn splendor. Front to back: rabbitbrush (*Ericameria nauseosa*), prairie aster (*Machaeranthera bigelovii*), amaranth (*Amaranthus cruentus*) and corn (*Zea mays*).

## Understanding Our Land

Robert Frost observed: "the land was ours before we were the land's." Those of us who live in the West have crisscrossed this land with barbed wire and roads, built sprawling cities and massive shopping centers, planted lush grass and thirsty trees to create an east coast or west coast look to our parks and gardens, even though we claim we love the austere western landscape that lured us here. We own the land, but the land has not yet claimed us.

Perhaps the first stage in having the land claim us is to understand our climatic region and the plant life that grows in it. Most people who live in Colorado are immigrants from other very different climates where many different plants grow. They find it difficult if not impossible to adjust their "secret garden" to the reality of Colorado. They have little knowledge and no frame of reference for the region in which they have put down roots.

After a rainless spell, and particularly in drought years, they find the Great Plains very stark. Some may not know that the "Great American Desert" was the name given to this area in 1819 by Stephen Long, leader of the third U.S. government expedition to the West. Travelers who came after Long eventually discovered that far drier regions—true deserts—were found to the south and west of the Rockies.

What are human transplants to make of the sparse grasslands of the High Plains? It may surprise them to learn that the grasslands that stretch across Eurasia from Hungary in the west to Manchuria in the Far East is the closest correlative to our native prairie. The Russian word *step'* (*steppe*) is now used to describe the cold winter, hot summer grasslands and shrub lands that lie across the heart of all the great continents: South America, Africa, Asia—and North America. In South America, many names have been applied to semiarid steppe including *puna* and the more familiar *pampas*, although much of the pampas are subtropical or warm temperate—closer to the ecosystem that ecologists usually class as savanna. At their southern and western extremities, the pampas are unquestionably steppe, however. South Africa has a wide swath of grassy highveld in the east that gradually transforms into the more arid karoo— paralleling the transition that occurs in the American West, starting with Midwestern tallgrass prairie through short grass prairie to sage lands in the Great Basin and Colorado Plateau.

Tangle of tall native annuals in tallgrass portion of Plains Garden including Rocky Mountain beeplant (*Cleome serrulata*) and common sunflower (*Helianthus annuus*).

Steppe climate regions are more sparsely settled than the wetter, more maritime portions of the countries where they occur. These regions nevertheless have played a pivotal role in human evolution: steppe has been the superhighway of animal migration and of the nomads who followed them. The various semiarid continental regions are not only visually similar, but many of the geographical features in each of these areas seem to uncannily echo the landforms elsewhere. Drop an unsuspecting person in the heart of Asia, South Africa, Argentina or Colorado and unless they recognize the flora, they will not know which continent they are on. All four great steppes share remarkable parallels in their biomes (the complex of living organisms found in an ecological region) and floristics (the relationship among plant types) as well. The grass, legume and aster families are the three largest families in each disparate region. Many of the lesser families are well represented in all four regions as well, including the figwort, mint and borage families. It is interesting to note these are the families that figure prominently in both vegetable and herb gardens (a clue perhaps that the history of human-plant interaction traces its origins to the steppe). Casual visitors to the Front Range, used to the lush forests of maritime regions, often assume that the flora in high, dry, continental regions is impoverished. They think that the steppe is barren and the soil is sterile. Nothing could be further from the truth. Because there is less rainfall here, far fewer nutrients are leached out of the soil than in areas that have greater rainfall. Soil scientists call prairie soils "pedocals."

There is enormous biodiversity in semiarid regions. Almost any random spot in Colorado has more species of plants per acre than comparable areas in the eastern United States. At this time, more than three thousand species of plants are known to be indigenous to Colorado, compared to a mere thousand species that originally grew in Great Britain—which has more than twice the area of Colorado. It's true that the Rocky Mountain tree flora is meager compared to Maryland, for example, but this imbalance is more than compensated for by the fantastic variety of smaller woody and herbaceous plants that vary so dramatically at each elevation and change abruptly as you travel around the West.

Is it any surprise that those who come here from other regions without knowledge of the steppe environment quickly become frustrated when they try to grow the plants they knew on either coast or in the more humid Midwest? When they dig, instead of rich black loam, they find stiff clay or loose sand in their Front Range gardens. The expensive tree they plant dies. They never seem to be able to water enough, and when they do, they often find themselves deluged in the rare but often soggy monsoon spells during which even moisture-loving plants can drown. Eventually, many new homeowners come to Denver Botanic Gardens to find out what they're doing wrong and to get advice and ideas about how to make their home landscaping not just prettier, but more durable. In short, they are looking for a way to understand the land they have claimed.

Aspen fleabane (*Erigeron speciosus*) in the Ponderosa Border portion of Western Panoramas.

## Claiming the Land by Education and Example

For much of the last half century, Denver Botanic Gardens was the only public garden of its kind between St. Louis and California (except for a few gardens in the desert Southwest). This vast expanse embraces some of the most gorgeous scenery and climatic juxtapositions on earth. Tourists and locals alike marvel at the natural wonders of Rocky Mountain National Park and other public lands with which our region is so richly endowed. A botanic garden seems not only to encourage stewardship of our precious wilderness, but also to guide the hand of mankind as we impact nature more and more.

Denver Botanic Gardens seeks to enlighten visitors about the many facets of the plant kingdom. It boasts the largest collection of plants from cold temperate continental regions in North America—and possibly in the world. Over the past two decades, the designers and horticulturists have developed seven distinctive gardens composed largely of plants of known wild provenance from Colorado and nearby states. These native and naturalistic gardens likely contain the finest collections of Rocky Mountain and Great Plains native plants in cultivation. They are unquestionably the jewels among our plant collections.

Vignette of Dryland Mesa, with Mojave sage (*Salvia pachyphylla*) and paperflower (*Psilostrophe tagetina*) providing summer-long color.

> The Gardens showcase the rich flora of semiarid climates around the globe that are correlative climates to Colorado…

But more than presenting an outstanding collection of plants, the Gardens showcase the rich flora of semiarid climates around the globe that are the correlative ("sister") climates to Colorado and provide both the new plants and the artistic models that homeowners can learn from in order to design a vibrant, year-round garden featuring native and adapted plants.

Coming to grips with the semiarid climate is step one. In 2002 the Denver metropolitan area received less than 7 inches of precipitation. The city imposed stringent watering restrictions on the residents; grassy areas in public parks and private lawns turned yellow in the rainless summer. It would not be an exaggeration to say that the metropolitan area population panicked—especially the 60,000 people in the region who depend on landscape construction, maintenance and plant sales for a living. Suddenly, Xeriscape® classes and seminars were being offered everywhere. So many people signed up for the classes that in some cases there were waiting lists to get into them.

Horned poppy (*Glaucium corniculatum*)

However, human nature is such that interest waned dramatically after the heavy snows and near-normal precipitation in 2003 and 2004. But tree rings and historical records prove that drought is the rule and not the exception in the Rocky Mountain region. To add to the problem, the population in Colorado has been doubling every few decades: a population in excess of 7 million may not be too many decades ahead. Water consumption for domestic needs will ultimately trump the use of water for both ornamental and agricultural purposes.

Unlike population, precipitation rates are not expected to rise. Currently, deep wells provide the water supply of many Front Range cities. It is worrisome that water tables are receding at much faster rates than forecasted. Some day, cities will need to tap into the already oversubscribed reservoirs. During severe droughts, irrigating gardens is perceived as a luxury. One of the characteristics of steppe climates is their unpredictability. An acute drought can often become prolonged, and then it is more than likely that permanent plantings—trees and shrubs as well as perennials—will perish in large numbers. We forget that vegetation generates unseen benefits: the effect of cooling by trees on cities would otherwise have to be offset by rising energy costs of increased air conditioning. Real estate agents know that landscaping has a significant impact on property values. The Rocky Mountains will not be nearly as attractive when the communities around them are dessicated and in the throes of drought panic.

10  GARDENING WITH ALTITUDE: *Cultivating a New Western Style*

# THE UNWATERED GARDEN

What if a drought occurred and nobody noticed? What if our gardens consisted of plants that were unfazed by drought years such as 2002 (incidentally, the driest year thus far recorded in Colorado)? If plants that thrive in hot, dry weather composed the bulk of regional gardens, drought would effectively cease to be an issue for all of us.

Denver Botanic Gardens has paved the way for this scenario by creating a number of gardens that are completely unwatered. Gardeners who have always assumed that beauty in gardens only results from copious use of the hose can see the fallacy in that statement by visiting several sites at the Gardens that do not even have irrigation systems: Dryland Mesa, Plains Garden, the steppe portion of June's PlantAsia and Anna's Overlook. Another five gardens (Western Panoramas, Wildflower Treasures, Sacred Earth, Gates Montane and Water-Smart gardens) are watered only a few times each growing season, depending on rainfall patterns. Similar water-smart garden techniques characterize Centennial Gardens – an artistic, beautiful design utilizing low water plants throughout, rather than in a zone separate from the rest of the garden.

Some fear that unwatered gardens will be dull or weedy looking. We beg to disagree. The dry gardens at Denver Botanic Gardens are diverse and interesting in all seasons. They range from highly naturalistic to semiformal in design, but all of them contain rich collections of beautiful plants arranged with great artistry. Thousands of kinds of plants have been tested in these gardens over the years, resulting in a rich palette of trees, shrubs and herbaceous plants that can be combined to create lush gardens requiring no supplemental water once established. These gardens are the workshop where a new, truly adapted and regional style of garden is being forged.

Glimpse of Dryland Mesa in high summer. Front to back: prairie zinnia (*Zinnia grandiflora*), rough agave (*Agave asperrima*), various prickly pear (*Opuntia* spp.) and desert willow (*Chilopsis linearis*).

Wildflower Treasures, featuring the Mount Evans trough in the foreground with old man of the mountain (*Tetraneuris grandiflora*) and cushion of alpine phlox (*Phlox condensata*).

# Research, Discover and Debut

I like to think that botanic gardens are a clearing to which people come to be inspired by the natural world that surrounds and nurtures us. To create such a clearing, the staff at Denver Botanic Gardens has concentrated its research on the rich flora of the Rockies and Intermountain region. Many plants new to the state—and even new to science—have been found on staff expeditions. Seed from exploration has been propagated and incorporated into more and more gardens, particularly the many gardens featuring native plants. Hundreds of native plants have had their horticultural debut at Denver Botanic Gardens. Twenty-five years ago it would have been difficult to find more than one or two kinds of penstemon, for example, at any local nursery. Today there are dozens of species available at some garden centers, and many more can be obtained by mail order. This process has been accelerated by the horticultural research conducted by the staff and the displays created at the Gardens.

A few examples of the many plants introduced by Denver Botanic Gardens include New Mexico figwort (*Scrophularia macrantha*), which was introduced from Luna County, New Mexico in 1992. It is considered the showiest species in its genus with two-inch waxy, tubular red flowers produced through the entire summer season. Rocky Mountain zinnia (*Zinnia grandiflora*) had its regional debut in the early 1980s in the Rock Alpine Garden from plants collected near Cañon City, Colorado. *Prunus pumila* var. *besseyi* Pawnee Buttes™ was collected by Gardens staff at about the same time and has become a popular groundcover all over North America over the past decade.

Right to left: yarrow (*Achillea* 'Terracotta'), tilted pot filled with cultivars of *Sempervivum* spp., tickseed (*Coreopsis verticillata* 'Moonbeam') and blue oat grass (*Helictotrichon sempervirens*) in background.

Denver Botanic Gardens has become an important venue for breeders throughout the region. It was here that the first public display promoted *Penstemon strictus* 'Bandera' (produced by the Los Lunas Plant Materials Center of the U.S. Conservation Service near Albuquerque, New Mexico) and *Penstemon digitalis* 'Husker Red' (developed by Dr. Dale Lindgren, University of Nebraska North Platte Experiment Station).

A less heralded achievement at the Gardens has been to raise awareness of the hardiness and ornamental potential of the immense palette of native American succulents and other native plants of the southwestern uplands. The Dryland Mesa has evolved into one of the largest collections of hardy American cacti, combined artfully with shrubs and wildflowers as they occur in nature. Horticulturist Dan Johnson designed a bold garden titled Yuccarama, featuring a large collection of woody lilies in this hot microclimate in the late 1990s. More than a dozen species of *Yucca* (many of them treeform), three species of *Hesperaloe*, *Agave* and several *Dasylirion* are combined with a wealth of showy dryland perennials to provide color and interest in all seasons. None of the plants in this dazzling garden were available commercially outside Texas or Arizona a few decades ago. Denver Botanic Gardens has greatly expanded the notion of what is hardy in the Zone 5 Denver area. We have been stunned to see so little snow or cold damage on these giant subtropical-seeming behemoths.

The concept of Xeriscape® and Water-Smart Gardening has evolved alongside the plant collections: one cannot design low-water gardens without plants that thrive in them. But plants are not enough; you must have artistic models to show people how to combine the plants effectively. The Gardens has provided both. The Water-Smart Garden, designed by renowned gardener Lauren Springer Ogden and refined and maintained by Dan Johnson, has been a stunning showcase of low-water plants combined with great artistry for year-round effect. Visitors note that water-smart gardens contain a much higher proportion of evergreen foliage plants that invariably look far better in the long winter months than traditional heavily watered landscapes where so many plants go completely dormant in winter: a compelling reason to dry out.

…Denver Botanic Gardens' horticulturists have gone on expeditions to Turkey, Pakistan and China, often bringing back seed to grow and observe.

## SURPRISING ASIAN PIONEERS

Plants from the true steppes of Asia (a "sister" climate of ours) make up a surprising proportion of flowers and trees used by the pioneers who settled the West. They still form the core of what is sold at local nurseries. Asian place names show up repeatedly on labels of plants sold and grown here: *amurensis, anatolica, asiatica, bucharica, chinensis, persica, sibirica, tatarica* and *tangutica* are some of the recurrent species epithets a gardener must learn in the West. Lilacs, bush honeysuckle (*Lonicera maackii*), shrub roses like Harison's yellow (*Rosa x harisonii*) and Austrian copper rose (*Rosa foetida*), tulips, irises and peonies—even annuals such as larkspur (*Consolida ajacis*)—all trace their ancestry to the windy plains of Eurasia. No wonder these have prospered so!

Many of Denver Botanic Gardens' horticulturists have gone on expeditions to Turkey, Pakistan and China, often bringing back seed to grow and observe. The bounty of Asia is yielding outstanding new plants that have captivated local gardeners. For example, Turkish veronica (*Veronica liwanensis*), one of the most successful new groundcovers in the region, was first collected by an expedition to northeastern Turkey in 1977 and introduced at the Gardens just a few years later. The prickly spikethrifts (*Acantholimon* spp.) have proven to be extremely drought-tolerant and long-lived; this genus provides a very showy display in sunny gardens. These and many other startling novelties are on display in June's PlantAsia, a horticultural cornucopia of the riches of Asia designed and built by horticulturist Mark Fusco and his associates.

Bamboo grove in June's PlantAsia, featuring path through *Phyllostachys nuda*, *P. glauca* and *P. aureosulcata*.

Glimpse of Asian groundcovers through moongate in June's PlantAsia: lilyturf (*Liriope muscari*), Japanese sedge (*Carex morrowii* 'Ice Dance').

*The South African border in high summer with torch lilies (*Kniphofia *'Alcazar' and* K. uvaria *'Royal Castle Hybrids') in full glory.*

## Hail the Hardy South Africans

South African plants have had a huge impact on horticultural thinking in Denver in recent decades: the genus *Delosperma* (ice plant) essentially did not exist in the horticultural literature in North America prior to the introduction and popularization of *D. nubigenum* and *D. cooperi* at Denver Botanic Gardens in the early 1980s. These have become the most popular-selling perennials at many garden centers, not only in Denver but throughout North America and even abroad. A dozen or more species of the same family have proven to have similar potential, all of them thus far hybridized or selected at the Gardens. D. 'Kelaidis' Mesa Verde™ is the most successful of these; it produces iridescent copper pink flowers over a long summer season. This variety, which occurred as a spontaneous hybrid at the Gardens, is now eagerly sought around the world.

These and a host of other hardy South Africans are displayed in the South African Plaza, probably the largest collection of plants from that continent found outside the subtropics. Other successful introductions from the karoo (an arid plateau of southern Africa) include little pickles (*Othonna capensis*), a succulent composite that blooms for five or more months in the garden. Several African daisies introduced by the Gardens, including species of hardy sundaisy (*Osteospermum*, *Arctotis* and *Gazania*) are becoming popular perennials in Zone 5 and even Zone 4 gardens where they were never before thought to be hardy. *Diascia* (twinspur) is often used as an annual even in mild climates, but *D. integerrima* Coral Canyon™ has proved to be versatile and very cold hardy. Denver Botanic Gardens is recognized as the institution that has truly pioneered the awareness of the extent and importance of South African plants to gardens throughout the cold temperate world.

South America has yet to have the impact on regional horticulture that the other regions have demonstrated thus far. The steppes of Patagonia are so rich in a wide diversity of showy flowers that this region may rival Africa one day as a source of outstanding and drought-tolerant introductions. I believe that plants from the higher, drier parts of the Andes will provide western gardens of the twenty-first century the same sort of pizzazz we now associate with South Africa: a whole new continent of possibilities.

*Aloe*

> …the genus *Delosperma* essentially did not exist in the horticultural literature in North America prior to the introduction and popularization of *D. nubigenum* and *D. cooperi* at Denver Botanic Gardens in the early 1980s.

Most of the Plant Select choices made their horticultural debut at Denver Botanic Gardens.

## A Guide for Consumers: Plant Select

A cooperative agreement between Denver Botanic Gardens, Colorado State University and nurseries across America is designed to bring plants better suited to North American garden conditions to the consumer. Plants are proposed to a Propagation Committee of Plant Select and distributed among cooperators for observation and testing. If the plant fulfills the many stringent expectations (showy flowers, good habit, ease of propagation) and if it is determined to pose no threat as an invasive, it may be one of a handful of plants introduced every spring to the public under the Plant Select imprimatur.

In 2006 there will be 64 types of different plants available at garden centers across the United States with Plant Select labels representing sales well over 6 million plants. Most of the Plant Select choices made their horticultural debut at Denver Botanic Gardens. Many are native western wildflowers, including many penstemons and daisies. A surprising number of plants in this program are evergreen or have attractive habit through the gardening season. Many, like the ice plants (*Delosperma*) or Red Rocks™ penstemon (*Penstemon* x *mexicali* Red Rocks™) or chocolate flower (*Berlandiera lyrata*), bloom throughout the growing season. The bulk of introductions tolerate protracted periods of drought, and many will grow without supplemental irrigation in the semiarid West. Plant Select, the most conspicuous result of the horticultural research conducted at the Gardens, has a direct impact on home gardeners locally and across the globe.

Native chocolate flower (*Berlandiera lyrata*) with South African Tanager™ gazania (*Gazania krebsiana* Tanager), both popularized by Plant Select.

Blue globe onion (*Allium caeruleum*)

Medley of wildflowers in the Rock Alpine Garden, including corn poppy (*Papaver rhoeas*) and blue globe onion (*Allium caeruleum*)

GARDENING WITH ALTITUDE: *Cultivating a New Western Style*

## Exquisite Design: An Essential Ingredient

Denver Botanic Gardens may be a great museum of plants, but the manner in which these plants are showcased is what perhaps distinguishes these Gardens from others around the nation and the world.

A number of world-renowned landscape architects have left their imprint on the master plan of the Gardens starting with Sacco DeBoer who designed the first garden, as well as parks throughout Denver and other cities across the West. This visionary architect who planted most of Denver's parkways was a great lover of rock work, and fittingly this first garden was built with monumental granite boulders recreating a quiet tribute to our foothills. Garrett Eckbo, a principal of EDAW (the largest landscape architecture firm in America) executed the first master plan for the Gardens. Eckbo was noted as a creator of the Western style, who mastered the outdoor living space and natural design. Ironically, he created a rather rectilinear, formal framework at the Gardens that has endured the test of time. His baton was passed on to Herb Schaal, also a principal of EDAW, who subsequently designed the highly naturalistic Rock Alpine Garden, a formal Rose Garden and the Sensory Garden. Schaal executed the redesign of the west pond in the Gates Montane Garden, a graceful, restful setting. America's preeminent architect of Japanese gardens, Koichi Kawana, created the Shofu-en in close collaboration with Kai Kawahara, who oversaw the collection installation of 178 remarkable ancient ponderosa pines (*Pinus ponderosa*) that are a signature of this Japanese garden.

Geoffey Rausch is a well-known Pennsylvania landscape architect who created the Romantic Gardens complex, although the plantings in the Schlessman Plaza and Fragrance Garden were largely the design of Lauren Springer Ogden, the best known garden writer and designer working in the region today. Springer Ogden also designed the Water-Smart Garden, South African Plaza and the grand O'Fallon Perennial Border along with Rob Proctor. Jane Silverstein Reis is revered as one of the most prolific residential designers in Denver history. She designed the Scripture Garden and created the conceptual design of the Plains Garden. Chris Moritz and Lou Hammer are regarded as two of the finest designers in Denver in the twentieth century. They created the shady Low Maintenance Garden, which is now incorporated into the eastern end of Woodland Mosaic. Rob Proctor, who served as horticultural director between 1999 and 2001, designed the Cutting Garden, Drop Dead Red Border and Wildflower Treasures. Gayle Weinstein, who preceded Rob in the 1980s as horticultural director, did the first draft of Dryland Mesa with Ken Ball (landscape architect with Denver Water), as well as the woody backbone of Birds and Bees. Tom Peace is a noted local author and designer who created the Mile High Border along York Street.

> A number of world-renowned landscape architects have left their imprint on the master plan of the Gardens…

The Cottonwood Border of Western Panoramas at dusk with cup plant (*Silphium perfoliatum*) and switch grass (*Panicum virgatum* 'Heavy Metal').

GARDENING WITH ALTITUDE: *Cultivating a New Western Style*

Last but not least, the horticulture staff at Denver Botanic Gardens has designed many of our very best gardens. Dan Johnson has created twelve distinct areas including the Western Panoramas, native gardens and the plantings for the El Pomar Waterway. Mark Fusco was instrumental in creating Wildflower Treasures, but entirely masterminded June's PlantAsia, the conifer berm extension and the Alpine Rock Garden at Mount Goliath. Ebi Kondo executed the final Monet Garden redesign, Victorian Secret Garden (with Dan Johnson), Shady Lane (with renowned gardener Marcia Tatroe) and the redesign of the May Bonfils-Stanton Memorial Rose Garden (with Loddie Dolinski) and the Kitchen Garden. Many other designers have at one time or another had a hand in one of the many gardens on the grounds or in the greenhouses.

Many major public gardens are the work of a handful of architects or designers whose style permeates the whole. This can appear very tasteful at first, but sometimes less interesting for the repeat visitor. Although only twenty-three acres in size, Denver Botanic Gardens seems to be far larger and the gardens all the more stimulating because of the manner in which the vision of different designers has been achieved and preserved.

Few public gardens contain such a diversity of garden styles containing utterly distinct collections. The wealth of cacti and dryland gardens stand out all the more starkly because of the serpentine waterways that curve and stretch out into numerous pools and rills and ponds—some sternly linear and others utterly natural from one end of the grounds to the other. The water gardens are a signature feature that attract great attention from visitors. These inspired the genesis of a worldwide movement in water gardening when the first water garden society formed here in 1983.

Some of the gardens were designed and installed a half century ago and have persisted almost unchanged. From time to time the Gardens are invaded: giant "insects" arrived with the Big Bugs display of 1999 and monumental stone sculptures came from Zimbabwe (Chapungu: *Custom and Legend, A Culture in Stone* exhibit in 2004). These changing exhibits allow the Horticulture Department to select certain themes and colors to provide cohesion throughout the 23 acres.

A symphony of succulents in Dryland Mesa
Thompson's yucca (*Yucca thompsoniana*) and Eve's needle
(*Y. faxoniana*) and dormant ocotillo (*Fouquieria splendens*)

Dwarf form of purple ice plant (*Delosperma cooperi*) in tipsy pots on Anna's Overlook.

The containers are a story unto themselves. Over the years the display has grown from a few dozen pleasant pots to an extravaganza of many hundreds of containers filled with lavish Edwardian designs in some gardens, or simple masses of annuals in another, or even tender succulents or hardy perennials. The container plantings are carefully placed each year to enhance the element of surprise for visitors. Pots are used to highlight seasonal themes and to provide focal points. One year they are brimming with showy annuals to celebrate the visit of All-America Selections to Denver. The next year severe drought inspires a bevy of succulent hanging pots and troughs, and yet another year most are filled with plants native to Africa to complement the African sculpture exhibit.

Although these gardens have been created over a half-century under several different master plans, a vital story of our local gardening scene unfolds, and perhaps something even more profound emerges as you wend your way through the Gardens. Each year the dramatic Crossroads container extravaganza adumbrates the theme of the year. You turn south through the grand O'Fallon Perennial Border and the impeccable Victorian era borders' carefully calibrated color schemes remind you that our horticulture scene is firmly rooted in western Europe. You progress through lavish Romantic Gardens, where vibrant color schemes and artistry prevail, and this theme is underscored. The intricate Elizabethan-style knot gardens in the Herb Garden transport you even deeper into the European garden tradition, hearkening to the Mediterranean.

From here, however, your journey takes you to more unusual garden styles and unique floristics. June's PlantAsia envelopes you in the vast wealth of the Asian flora and ancient Chinese gardening style, including a compact version of the Central Asian steppe. And soon you are thrust on sunny plazas blazing with exotic African color and then onto a sunswept desert butte bristling with cacti and wind-sculpted junipers. The Rock Alpine Garden can transport you to the tundra any time of year. Or you can sit by a large pond surrounded by wildflowers or at the nearby Monet Cafe looking down on Victoria waterlilies (*Victoria cruziana*) and lotuses (*Nelumbo* cvs.) with a panoramic view of eleven distinct gardens, each with its own palette of plants and story to tell. By the time you have reached the billowing prairie grasses in the Laura Smith Porter Plains Garden you have transected much of the legacy of world horticulture. Your journey should end at the grand Western Panoramas, which provide a coda. Here native plants are combined in grand, romantic sweeps that celebrate our local horticultural bounty in symphonic fashion.

Indoors you can luxuriate in a lowland tropical rainforest or admire a wealth of epiphytes on a Cloud Forest Tree. Each garden outdoors or under glass contains its own distinctive palette of plants combined, however, in a clear artistic vehicle that is the vision of an artistic designer in partnership with the extraordinary horticulturist who inherits and cherishes the garden subsequently.

I never cease to marvel at how different the mood is in the early morning (when you can often see foxes scampering about) to the hot, sometimes glaring midday sun. Late afternoon is a magic time in any garden, but at Denver Botanic Gardens when the vast sky overhead turns apricot pink and the mountains are silhouetted in dark purple, the gardens positively glow in the light like a fairyland. The colors everywhere are electrifying on cool, overcast days when magenta, yellow or orange leaps out at you like neon at night. Few garden pictures are as pleasing as the ancient bonsai pines in the Japanese Garden (Shofu-en) nestling fluffy snow on their black branches on a sunny winter day. Each stroll is utterly unique. A visit to Denver Botanic Gardens is invariably full of surprises arousing a boundless sense of wonder. For the attentive visitor, each stroll unfolds a new view and a whole new vision of our horticultural heritage.

Thousands of homeowners have studied these gardens, attended classes and symposia and are taking the lessons of Water-Smart Gardening back to their gardens. Meanwhile, the staff members seek out the most beautiful plants from the world's high, cold and dry regions, testing and researching them systematically and finding ways to make these plants succeed at Denver Botanic Gardens and eventually in your garden beyond your wildest expectations. Day after day, hundreds of visitors and busloads of children wander through the borders, drinking in the magic of color and sensory stimulation that is a garden. We hope this garden will become their personal secret garden that will inspire them far into the future.

Black-eyed Susan (*Rudbeckia hirta*) with meadow sage (*Salvia pratensis*) and torch lilies (*Kniphofia* 'Cobra') in the Mile High Border.

# GOING NATIVE IN THE GARDENS

By Dan Johnson

*...The full impact of the Front Range now leapt into view, from the hulking outline of Pikes Peak in the south, stretching northward to the reclining foothills beyond Fort Collins...*

Sunflowers gild the rural roads of Boulder County.

Photograph–Dan Johnson

June 15, 1981. I had been driving for three days, and now a scorching dry heat blasted through my open car windows. According to the map, Boulder was only some sixty miles away. Where were the mountains? I had grown agonizingly familiar with the slow rise and fall of the highway as I crested each endless wave of grass. *So much grass!* Where else can one seem to be creeping along at 80 miles per hour? The view was nearly the same the day before, as I had sailed past rich emerald farms and tall waving grasses of eastern Kansas. Yet here it was different. The greens were more subdued and washed with silver and tan, the grasses hanging on for dear life, shaking short and rigid against a stiff wind. Isolated windmills and water tanks anchored spidery webs of cattle trails. Through the heat, far-off cottonwood trees shimmered in slender green lines along the shallow banks of the Platte River, all bowing eastward and murmuring among themselves against the dry incessant wind.

Seen with unfamiliar eyes, the searing endlessness of it all leaves a tangible gnaw in one's soul, a longing for safe retreat that pushes one forward. Here Earth's fragile skin is stretched taut and chapped between receding horizons. This landscape is the "Great American Desert" that early nineteenth-century pioneers deemed hostile and worthless. Its only potential was to be tamed, reclaimed and civilized. This, I thought, is the reason easterners stay east, and westerners stay west.

The sun was inching toward the western horizon amid high cotton clouds. A vague, hazy drift hung low along the skyline, and now in the lower light, distant hills finally became distinct from the clouds skidding overhead. Mountains at last! They drew closer at a snail's pace, line and shadow taking form with each passing mile. Distant snowfields glinted in the lowering sun, and farms once again peppered the rolling prairie around me. It was easy, almost necessary, to forget the vast grasslands I had just skimmed over. One more rise in the highway, and my vision was brought up short by the great divide of the Rockies. The full impact of the Front Range now leapt into view, from the hulking outline of Pikes Peak in the south, stretching northward to the reclining foothills beyond Fort Collins—an impossible span of more than a hundred miles. Boulder's Flatirons vaulted skyward at the prairie edge, and the crags of the Indian Peaks stood in crisp silhouette against salmon-tinted clouds. Home at last.

GARDENING WITH ALTITUDE: *Cultivating a New Western Style*

The high and dry San Luis Valley shimmers with the late-summer gold of rabbitbrush (*Ericameria* ssp.).

Going Native In The Gardens

Photograph–Dan Johnson

## Large Doses of Reality

Mine was not a new experience; it was the inevitable disconnect between the newcomer and the unfamiliar. Established tastes and tradition can leave little room for innovation or new ideas. Early on in Colorado's history, *survival* in a harsh land was paramount—there was little room for error. Farming here was a challenge even in good times, and in the nineteenth and early twentieth centuries, settlers learned quickly that different approaches were necessary. During this period in the mountain West, gardening for pleasure was secondary at best, a luxury indulged primarily by the wealthy and steeped in the traditions of the East. In homage to cities like Boston and Chicago, grand tree-lined avenues bound affluent neighborhoods against the frontier rather than uniting them with the surrounding wild lands and vistas.

Even now, with only one hundred or so years of "gardening" behind us, the patterns are set. For many, it still is difficult to see beyond tradition and to embrace the look and feel of the natural western landscape. Certainly we appreciate the wild landscape—in its place, out "there" somewhere beyond our cities and towns—but it has seldom been the inspiration for our own garden designs. Little if any clamor is heard when pristine prairies or foothill meadows are dozed away in an instant to make way for another brand-x mart or "single family unit." And sadly, no landscape is more yielding than the fragile short-grass prairie. Self-sustaining natural gardens and priceless scenery are replaced in an instant with unsustainable landscapes that would perish in a matter of weeks without their life-support systems of poly pipe and valves and diverted water.

"...sadly, no landscape is more yielding than the fragile shortgrass prairie." A view of a Front Range community.

Reality can come in large doses. Much of Colorado's early settlement flourished during the relatively wet years between 1905 and 1929. The 1930s brought the Dust Bowl and a rude awakening to a primarily agrarian population. Since then, agriculture has adapted greatly to the reality that drought is standard fare throughout the West. However, when the drought of 1976-1977 struck, a growing urban population and a burgeoning tourist and ski industry felt the impact in new ways. Economies were strained and lawns went brown. Suddenly the myth of endless and abundant water was dashed.

It was not a shock to everyone. Some had said for years that we were engaged in a battle with nature that we could never really win. Still, we strove for decades to replicate the verdant landscapes of the coasts. Now a compelling reality turned the focus inward—the climate demanded it.

As so often happens, the crisis passed, and by the 1980s wetter weather had dulled the urgency felt by so many during the throes of drought. Gardeners, for the most part, were no exception. Rain or shine, the soft hiss of irrigation whispered through luxuriant neighborhoods once again.

Savvy gardeners had taken notice, however. Drought would happen again. Water reserves were finite and the population was increasing. The current pace was unsustainable, even with new water and drought monitoring underway. And did traditional methods of gardening make sense anyhow? Was it wise to "battle against nature?" Did we need to water every square inch of garden every day? Couldn't we adapt just a bit to the reality of where we live?

Prairie coneflower (*Ratibida columnifera*)

Lead plant (*Amorpha canescens*)

A quiet retreat beneath whispering cottonwoods (*Populus deltoides* ssp. *monilifera*).

## A Taste of the Untamed

In the early days of the 1980s, Denver Botanic Gardens was already well respected for its vast collections and cutting-edge designs. With its tropical mystique, the Boettcher Tropical Conservatory had drawn people for nearly twenty years. Ever-changing display gardens brought waves of color each spring and summer. The newly completed Japanese Garden and Rock Alpine Garden had received international acclaim.

Early summer along the Water-Smart Garden path.

Thompson's yucca (*Yucca thompsoniana*)

Lace hedgehog cactus (*Echinocereus reichenbachii*)

> The Gardens has always been a public institution dedicated to education, stewardship and horticultural leadership.

Foxtail barley (*Hordeum jubatum*) drapes over blackfoot daisy (*Melampodium leucanthum*).

Photograph-Dan Johnson

Yet even at Denver Botanic Gardens little residual evidence existed of the water crisis of the mid-seventies. Only a few scattered plots of native plants were sprinkled through the gardens, and no large gardens were dedicated to the theme of water conservation. Traditional collections of roses and peonies and annual bedding plants held a powerful grip over most of the twenty-three acres.

Still, an awareness was dawning and plans were underway. The Gardens has always been a public institution dedicated to education, stewardship and horticultural leadership. Change was needed, and the first step was obvious: show people where they live.

The Laura Smith Porter Plains Garden came to fruition in 1983. It was conceived and created by Gayle Weinstein, along with Gardens staff and volunteers, as a tribute to one of Colorado's early settlers, Laura Smith Porter. Its purpose was to give city dwellers a sample of what Denver had been like a century ago: a wide open prairie where slight changes in topography, soil and exposure fostered a subtle diversity in native drought-tolerant plant communities. It was an immediate success, and thanks to the forethought and early work in this effort, the essential elements of this garden still flourish with only occasional intervention.

Many people found resonance with this garden and realized great satisfaction in creating patches of "prairie" in dry corners of a backyard or in narrow street-side strips where bluegrass routinely scorched in the summer sun. But it was not for everyone. In fact, municipalities often took a dim view of such "gardens," insisting that only uniformly coiffed blocks of well-watered green were acceptable.

The Laura Smith Porter Plains Garden has an untamed style that is hard for some to embrace. Occasionally, visitors can still be heard to mutter, "I wonder when they plan to do something with this area." Here, grasses and wildflowers run riot, presenting a vision quite incongruous with the concept most people still hold of what a garden "should" look like. Left largely to their own devices, plants move about the garden, seeding into their preferred niches and crowding up against their neighbors as they might in nature, with an ebb and flow dictated by the season at hand and the whims of weather. Seasonal highlights of lemon yellow or blazing red and purple broaden the color pallet, but the connotation is that of our natural landscapes. "Green" as most gardeners know it, is a fleeting experience in this garden as it is in nature.

This innovative garden unwittingly marked the beginning of a profound shift in the tenor of regionally attuned horticulture. Out of its success an effort arose to transform the basics of gardening in the arid West, with a degree of sensitivity to the demands of a high plains climate. Gardens were compartmentalized into wetter zones and drier zones. Plantings were modified to include more drought-tolerant plants. For the first time, the everyday gardener might consider the usefulness of native plants—a realm previously limited to a few eccentric gardeners on the fringe. Soil preparation and the use of mulches and efficient irrigation were encouraged and vast sweeps of thirsty lawn were scaled back to more conservative proportions.

Through the efforts of Denver Water and the landscape and gardening industry, a new word had been buzzing about. "Xeriscape" was born of the indisputable need to adjust our gardening style and habits to the reality of where we live. Denver Botanic Gardens expanded its efforts to provide the first real example of what a "xeriscape" could entail. With visionary design and innovative use of western native plants, the world's first Xeriscape Demonstration Garden came into being in 1986. A unique garden began to take shape, based on the original "seven principles" of xeriscape design. From its inception this garden also seemed destined to be rather untamed, with an informal style drawn more from the dominant ecosystems of the interior West than from familiar garden tradition. Many dozens of unique western plants that had rarely been seen in public or private gardens before now thrived along its rock ledges and grassy glades.

Rocky Mountain penstemon (*Penstemon strictus*)

However, by the mid-1990s even the native gardens at Denver Botanic Gardens had suffered their share of neglect. Nearly 20 wetter than usual years had lured many back into the realm of more traditional gardens, so prairie and xeriscape gardens had been left to fend for themselves. Weeds had gained a foothold and aggressive species like tansy aster (*Machaeranthera* spp.) and western wheatgrass (*Pascopyrum smithii*) had run rampant over the more timid gems of the gardens.

Several things became evident at this time. One was the need to renovate these existing gardens with both collection diversity and a new artistry in mind. Also, weeds needed immediate and ongoing control. In addition, a new infusion of species that had been lost, or nearly so, was key, as so much of the allure of these gardens is their diversity of form and texture, and the dramatic differences they present from one season to the next.

New opportunities and a fresh awareness began to emerge from these efforts. Sunny, dry gardens with boulders, various aspects and well-drained soils provide an endless range of niches and microclimates, just as the same features in natural landscapes would. The concept of "microclimates" still seems a revelation to some, but the term has been tossed about since at least the early 1960s, and the concept has been in evidence since man's earliest interactions with the earth and agriculture. The way it manifests itself is relatively simple: in Denver's zone 5 climate, pockets of zone 6 and even 7 exist in the sun-warmed shelter of urban structures or southeast facing slopes, especially here on the leeward side of the Rockies. When provided with good drainage and a sunny slope, these areas are especially suited to many of the drought-loving plants from our desert southwest, most of which had been deemed "too tender" to be grown on the high plains. Likewise, a cool north-facing niche, provided with organic soil and just a bit of moisture, might be an ideal spot for trilliums and perhaps a hardy azalea or Japanese maple (*Acer japonicum*).

With water conservation as a major goal, our focus turned more toward drought-loving desert and Mediterranean plants. Trials with a few "tender" plants like red-flower yucca (*Hesperaloe parviflora*), Parry's agave (*Agave parryi*) and beavertail pricklypear (*Opuntia basilaris*) had proven promising through the 1980s, but such novelties were often hard to locate, and investment in such risky plants was attempted only by a few curious home-gardeners and botanic gardens. Now more and more nurseries and plant propagators began looking to native plants as a potential source of revenue and a way to capitalize on the burgeoning interest in drought-tolerant and native gardening.

Claret cup cactus (*Echinocereus triglochidiatus*)

GARDENING WITH ALTITUDE: *Cultivating a New Western Style*

New Mexico agave (*Agave parryi* ssp. *neomexicana*)

Ten-petal blazing star (*Mentzelia decapetala*)

Photograph-Dan Johnson

With this improving availability and a renewed commitment to native plants from all parts of the arid West, our plant trials increased significantly. The planting of dozens of cacti, yucca and agave species stretched the limits of what was believed to be hardy here. Nearly unknown in Colorado gardens, plants like New Mexico agave (*Agave parryi* ssp. *neomexicana*), golden pricklypear (*Opuntia aurea*) and sacahuista (*Nolina microcarpa*) thrived with no supplemental watering and added a bold sculptural element not achieved by most hardy perennials. The burnt orange and coral of sunset hyssop (*Agastache rupestris*) became a mainstay of regional landscaping. Hailing from the east slope of the Sierra Nevada, little-known Mojave sage (*Salvia pachyphylla*) with its pungent ever-silver leaves and dusky rose-purple flowers was first grown here in 1998. It sailed through the drought of 2002 without a drop of irrigation and has since been chosen as a fantastic new Plant Select introduction.

As the Xeriscape Demonstration Garden has matured over the years, it has become a tribute to the durable plants and dry "grandscapes" of the West, not simply a clustering of similar plants or an homage to mulch and irrigation. In fact, by 1997, the irrigation in this garden and the adjacent Plains Garden was suspended completely with the infrequent exception made for new plantings. Two years later the name of the Xeriscape Demonstration Garden was changed to the Dryland Mesa: a title more evocative of wild western terrain and its unique plant communities. Now, after eight years of no irrigation, the plants have retained their compelling natural attributes and they continue to thrive and flower through all the vagaries of our changing weather.

Two South African gems for the dry garden: *Gazania krebsiana* Tanager™ with *Delosperma* 'John Proffitt'.

## A Smarter Garden

In the meantime, homeowners and landscape designers often saw the concept of gardening with native plants as an "all or nothing" endeavor. They planted either an exclusively native garden or a traditional garden, with rarely any overlap. Such efforts usually took the form of a shapeless "meadow" mish-mash that confused the onlooker. These native gardens, often relegated to back alleys or wasted areas that were seldom used, were frequently doomed to failure, as weeds and neglect left them no better off than any previous attempts. Even the most xeric native gardens need some care!

What was needed was the creation of a broad new garden style that focused almost entirely on plants known to have a similar and strong affinity for drier garden conditions: not just drought-tolerant, but drought-*loving*. Early images of xeriscape had become tainted with what some felt were negative stereotypes. The concept seemed rooted in deprivation, having to "go without" the lush green luxuriance people so often associate with a "real garden" and settling for only a tiny oasis of green while surrounding beds of gravel and cacti simmer in near-Saharan heat.

This new evolution in style required a smarter garden with more reasonable needs and no apologies for its lack of *Rhododendron* or *Astilbe*. These plants needed to thrive in dry conditions with every bit as much vigor and seasonal color as a conventional garden, and using the full range of characteristics of such plants: silvery foliage, succulent forms, spiked leaves and frothy, wiry textures. This garden needed to live on only occasional supplemental water (or none at all!) and it needed the broadest palette of plants possible, from nearly every continent. It needed to celebrate the look and feel of the arid West, and similar regions of the world, and find expression in the same palette of colors and textures that make the natural western landscapes so compelling. After all, newcomers were flocking to the arid West precisely because of its crisp air, its vast sun-drenched landscapes and wide open sweeps of sage, gold and tan under rainless skies. So why should people insist on changing the very nature of the place they claim to love? This garden celebrated a sense of place in a rich and welcoming way that had not been done at most botanic gardens up until then.

*This garden celebrated a sense of place in a rich and welcoming way…*

In the Water-Smart Garden at Denver Botanic Gardens, native buckwheat (*Eriogonum* spp.), *Yucca* and California poppies (*Eschscholzia californica*) thrive alongside Mediterranean and Asian *Salvia*, *Stachys* and *Marrubium*.

From the original Laura Smith Porter Plains Garden to the Xeriscape Demonstration Garden, and now to the Water-Smart Garden, each progressive endeavor represented a large forward shift in awareness, practicality and experimentation. Dozens of plants thought to be too tender for our climate actually thrived in the drier conditions of our Water-Smart Garden. A cast of unknowns now rushed onto center stage. Gardens luminary Panayoti Kelaidis had brought us the hardy South African ice plants just a year or two earlier. The new garden helped convey them to millions of gardeners across the continent. *Salvia* from arid parts of Europe and Asia and grasses and *Hesperaloe* from Mexico grew side by side with Mediterranean thymes and lavenders. The garden exceeded expectations. It set a new standard and drew visitors in, giving them fresh options that reached out to embrace the aesthetics of our natural landscapes while also proffering a rich array of color and texture and adventure in cultivating unique new plants.

Native plants still ran the show in the Plains and Xeriscape gardens, but in the new Water-Smart Garden they initially acted only as "extras." As experimentation continued, many more found a place here as well. The prevailing attitude—that with native plants, it was "all or nothing"—was being slowly laid to rest. Many western natives and their selected cultivars were thriving in other gardens, and adding them to this mix unleashed a host of new combinations scarcely considered in most Colorado landscapes. Autumn sage (*Salvia greggii*) had been grown in Colorado as an annual, but hardier forms were tested and proven to thrive in our hot summers and dry winters. Parry's agave (*Agave parryi*) had lived here for at least fifteen years. Now the list of *Agave* proven hardy in our sunny microclimates had reached a dozen or more, and they bristled up through carpets of pink creeping thyme (*Thymus serpyllum* 'Pink Chintz') and the early blooms of netted iris (*Iris reticulata*). Luminous violet spires of scarlet bugler (*Penstemon barbatus* 'Prairie Dusk') shimmered above the explosive lavender heads of Persian onion (*Allium christophii*). Ivory banners of waxen Thompson's yucca (*Yucca thompsoniana*) flowers towered among orange and gold foxtail lilies (*Eremurus stenophyllus*). This new convergence of natives and exotics was precisely the element that had been largely absent from most garden design: the unabashed fusion of the natural Western aesthetic with the best of what horticulture has to offer.

Giant flowering onion (*Allium giganteum*) sway in front of Thompson's yucca (*Yucca thompsoniana*).

Golden foxtail lilies (*Eremurus stenophyllus*) rise behind the white blooms of Mediterranean silver sage (*Salvia argentea*).

*Penstemon cobaea* x *P. triflorus*

Blanket Flower (*Gaillardia aristata*)

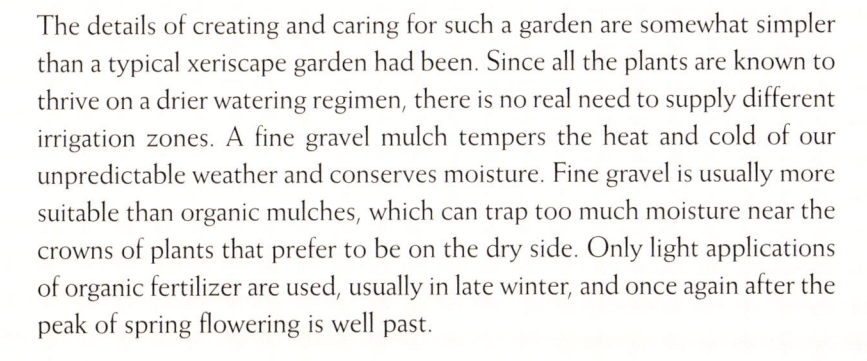

The details of creating and caring for such a garden are somewhat simpler than a typical xeriscape garden had been. Since all the plants are known to thrive on a drier watering regimen, there is no real need to supply different irrigation zones. A fine gravel mulch tempers the heat and cold of our unpredictable weather and conserves moisture. Fine gravel is usually more suitable than organic mulches, which can trap too much moisture near the crowns of plants that prefer to be on the dry side. Only light applications of organic fertilizer are used, usually in late winter, and once again after the peak of spring flowering is well past.

The weeds that choose to populate a dry garden can vary widely. A handful of annual weeds are the main offenders, namely cheatgrass (*Bromus tectorum*), groundsel (*Senecio vulgaris*) and henbit (*Lamium amplexicaule*). All will germinate, grow, flower and seed in cool damp weather from fall until spring, and their lively green stands out amid the dormant silver and tan of the Water-Smart Garden. Their color alone makes them easy to find—and remove—on those mild sun-warmed days of late winter and spring when we're already itching to get out and garden. They seldom germinate later in the heat of spring and summer, so eliminating them early gets us ahead of the game a bit. Each plant removed at this time, before seed has formed, reduces the seed bank in the soil and prevents the formation of many thousands of new seeds, greatly reducing future weed infestations. It is also a great time to take stock of how well the garden is coping with the stresses of winter and to reset any young plants that may have been frost-heaved from their beds.

Selecting the best plants for a water-smart garden is an adventure that sets one onto a surprising learning curve. With careful attention to microclimates, it is easy to meet the different needs of a wide range of plants. In our Water-Smart Garden, agaves, yuccas and cacti occupy many of the hot spots. Native shrubs like lead plant (*Amorpha canescens*) and Apache plume (*Fallugia paradoxa*) give the backdrop structure against a foil of existing piñon pines. Upright junipers and hardy forms of Arizona cypress (*Cupressus arizonica*) add strong vertical accents. Bearded *Iris*, *Solidago* and *Verbascum* fill sections where moisture is likely to linger a bit longer. Grasses like Mexican feather grass (*Nassella tenuissima*) and giant sacaton (*Sporobolus wrightii*) soften the scene with year-round movement and fine texture. Wild buckwheat (*Eriogonum* spp.) and sea lavender (*Limonium* spp.) create pastel drifts of lemon and violet, and carefree California poppies (*Eschscholzia californica*) seed about the garden in waves of neon orange.

Even through the worst years of our recent drought in 2002, the Water-Smart Garden was only watered seven times all year…

## A Cycle in Sync with Nature

The first flowers to appear each year are the earliest of spring bulbs. Hundreds of bulbs thrive with our cycle of late winter/early spring moisture, followed by summer heat and drier conditions. Species *Crocus* and netted iris (*Iris reticulata*) cultivars can surface as early as late January and February. In March and April, colorful species tulips open wide on sunny days, and short-lived yucca-like rosettes of Foxtail lily (*Eremurus* cvs.) foliage appear, to be followed by their foxtail blooms in May and June. Ornamental onions (*Allium* cvs.) appear early as well, and different species come into bloom from April to July, with most drying out to leave ornamental tan "sparklers" for weeks or months of interest.

Each season brings an entirely new look as perennials pass from peak bloom to decorative seedheads to dormant tan and silver. Hardy orange gazania (*Gazania krebsiana* Tanager™) will bloom on a sunny warm day even in the depths of winter, but will be ablaze in hot orange from late March through most of the spring and summer. Dianthus, poppies and cutleaf sage (*Salvia jurisicii*) present a rainbow of pink, orange and rich purple in May and June. The spires of a dozen penstemon varieties lend height to the mix, and their rattley seedheads can remain well into the winter.

By midsummer the jewel-toned Russian sage (*Perovskia atriplicifolia*) and hyssop (*Agastache* spp.) blend in shades of soft violet blue and smoky orange and raspberry. Late summer brings a transformation as the exuberance of spring is tempered by the mounting heat. Steely blue stems of bluestem joint fir (*Ephedra equisetina*) frame the foreground of common sunflowers in lemon and gold. Creamy panicles of fernbush (*Chamaebatiaria millefolium*) are abuzz with honeybees. Blue-mist spirea (*Caryopteris* cvs.) echoes the summer blue sky.

Desert four o'clock (*Mirabilis multiflora* var. *glandulosa*)

Photograph-Dan Johnson

Gardening with altitude: *Cultivating a New Western Style*

Fall brings a sense of rest and maturity to the garden. Seedheads steal the show with rusty, mounded buckwheat (*Eriogonum* spp.) lying casually against the soft sage green of horehound (*Marrubium rotundifolium*). White domed cushions of German statice (*Goniolimon tataricum*) shimmer next to the wooly silver rosettes of silver sage (*Salvia argentea*). Cacti are adorned with plump cherry-red fruits that persist into winter. Some cacti prosper all year in large containers that offer easy care and maintenance. Set above the tangle of neighboring plants, these containers act as living garden sculpture all year long, and capped with snow, they provide a bold component to the winter scene.

In the crisp, dry air of the West, winter brings a distinctive season of interest. Many grasses and seed stalks that would turn to mush in wetter coastal climes will freeze-dry where they stand. No need to clear-cut the garden in autumn as one might elsewhere. They persist, lending warm tones and textures for months, tall and defiant against winter wind and snow. By February and March, they are selectively thinned and removed, and as the first golden crocus emerge through fleeting spring snows, a new season begins.

Our Water-Smart Garden stretches south-facing along the full length of the Boettcher Tropical Conservatory, where it bakes in the summer heat and endures wide swings in temperature all year, but its rugged water-wise troop of plants has proven itself over time. Unlike our Dryland Mesa and Plains Garden, which thrive without any supplemental water, this garden needs an occasional deep soaking, but these plants actually perform their best when kept on a leaner diet of water and fertilizer. Too much of either, and they languish and flop under their own weight. Even through our recent drought in 2002, the Water-Smart Garden was only watered seven times all year, receiving about an inch and a half (or less) of water each time – far less than most conventional gardens require.

Succulent prickly pear fruits (*Opuntia phaeacantha* var. *major*) ripen behind the soft rusty sprays of wild buckwheat (*Eriogonum jamesii*).

Photograph-Dan Johnson

## Mainstreamed at Last

With the bonds of conventional gardening loosened a bit, other possibilities began to present themselves. A new interest in mainstreaming native plants had opened the door to creating a natural style in the heart of Denver Botanic Gardens—a look that could be immediately distinguished from that of Philadelphia or Chicago or New York. Four borders surrounded the large amphitheater where so many of the Gardens' events and activities take place. At the north edge, the Water-Smart Garden was one of these, and plants from the far corners of the world were thriving alongside a new infusion of western natives. What if we could create something new with natives, something we had never attempted before? In this large open space, how might we craft panoramic new borders that would unite the essence of the Western landscape with the artistry of an urban garden?

Flanking the other three sides of the amphitheater, three fresh borders were conceived, each highlighting one of Colorado's signature trees, with many of the natives that would accompany them in nature, and in a casual style reminiscent of their natural habitats. Yet they would not be strict "revegetations," or even replications of these habitats. We had already done that in the Plains Garden where the plants, a less select mix of natives, ran the show and moved about as they wished.

Several seasons earlier, a survey of our wildflowers at the Gardens gave us valuable information regarding the main season of bloom for more than 250 species. Now this information would be put to practical use, as we would use only the best and most ornamental of these natives. And since our political borders are a contrived artifice with no reflection of native ecosystems or plant communities, we would not restrict ourselves to Colorado natives alone, but would use plants from the region surrounding us as well. Meandering paths and rock outcrops would lend a relaxed, natural style. Wildflowers would grow, not in a wild free-for-all, but gathered into large drifts with an eye toward more traditional garden border techniques. Simple layers of grass would embrace swaths of color, short grasses in the foreground and tall plants in the back. A unique palette of plants would make each border distinct.

The plains cottonwood (*Populus deltoides* ssp. *monilifera*) was chosen to anchor the new border on the west side of the amphitheatre. As the only large trees actually native to Denver, they have long been a symbol of oasis and survival on the shortgrass prairie. In our Cottonwood Border they have rooted deeply and now soar above waves of blue grama grass (*Bouteloua gracilis*), desert four o'clock (*Mirabilis multiflora* var. *glandulosa*) and prairie winecups (*Callirhoe involucrata*). Each of these borders has its own style and its own watering needs. The cottonwoods and their prairie companions require very little supplemental irrigation, so this section receives only occasional deep watering.

Tufted seeds of Apache plume (*Fallugia paradoxa*).

Where the Great Plains and the Rockies collide, cottonwoods (*Populus deltoides* ssp. *monilifera*)
paint the prairies gold against the dark evergreen backdrop of ponderosa pines (*Pinus ponderosa*) near Boulder, CO.

Ponderosa pines (*Pinus ponderosa*) grace the foothill and montane zone of most of our western mountain ranges, from rugged canyon walls to fragrant open parklands. In the east border of the amphitheatre, the dappled light beneath ponderosa pines shelters Oregon grape holly (*Mahonia repens*) and the delicate blue bells of rock clematis (*Clematis columbiana* var. *tenuiloba*). Penstemons in red and violet lure hummingbirds to the sunny glades. The Ponderosa Border has become well established, but at this elevation we seldom receive the amount of precipitation they might enjoy in nature. Regular deep watering during the height of summer seems to serve them well.

Among the oldest living things on Earth, bristlecone pines (*Pinus aristata*) survive with tenacity on craggy wind-torn ridges that ply the heavens. Though nowhere common, they are adaptable survivors, coping with intense sun and drought, even in lower elevation gardens. Our south border, with bristlecone pines scattered along a rocky ridge above well-drained slopes, features the most adaptable and colorful of subalpine wildflowers. Rocky Mountain columbines (*Aquilegia caerulea*) and Idaho fescue (*Festuca idahoensis*) cover open meadows and harebells (*Campanula rotundifolia*) nestle in rock crevices. In their habitat, they would receive more precipitation than either ponderosas or cottonwoods. Moisture runs deep alongside the boulders and is retained near the surface by gritty gravel mulch. Careful planting helps to shade and cool the soil, so it requires only slightly more irrigation than the Ponderosa Border. Though not irrigation-free, all these borders demand far less water than most conventional borders.

Planted in the year 2000, these borders each have a long season of bloom, and grasses and seedheads persist long after for year-round appeal. In this setting the true character of many natives is shown to its best advantage. The rusty autumn-rose of little bluestem (*Schizachyrium scoparium*); shimmering billows of silver beardgrass (*Bothriochloa laguroides* ssp. *torreyana*); luminous silvery spikes of gayfeather (*Liatris punctata*) seed: all might have punctuated the plains garden, but here, in broad swathes backlit by a waning winter sun, they create a spectacle. Our native palette of trees, shrubs, grasses and perennial wildflowers has finally come home to the heart of the Gardens in a space we call the Western Panoramas.

The vast and primal topography of our deserts and grasslands have a powerful simplicity of style, and a complexity of composition…

## Simplicity of Style, Complexity of Composition

After my first long journey across the plains to the Front Range, living in Boulder County was a dream. Nearly 18 months passed before I ventured onto the prairie again. It's not that my experience had been unusually traumatic. In fact, it was probably quite typical for a newcomer. There simply was no reason to go back out there. Surrounded by the convenience of civilization and wrapped snugly in the lush green arms of Boulder, why would I go east? If there was time and opportunity, I headed up the steep canyons to the west to revel in the glorious heights of the Rockies.

Hindsight. Times and interests change. I have no regrets over my adolescent infatuation with Colorado's high country. It *is* magnificent, and it still compels and inspires me, but there is strength in diversity, and over time, new sensibilities can take hold of one's heart and conscience.

Living along the Front Range feels different to me now. In Denver and its surrounding communities, well-watered landscapes, golf courses and suburbs plod up and down along the edge of the mountains oblivious to the reality of where they are. This is high prairie, or at least it was: a near-desert steppe bathed year round in intense sunlight and catapulted from one season to the next in a matter of hours by wild swings in temperature and ferocious winds. Rainfall typically averages about 15 inches, but some years as little as 7 or as much as 24.

Colorado's predominantly dry steppe climate has more in common with the desert and Mediterranean climates to our south and west than with the soggy climates of the East and Northwest. Still, few of us have looked to this reality when searching for garden inspiration. Most want to emulate the leafy, moss-draped maritime climates of the east and west coasts, or look still further to Britain or Japan. In style and design much may be gained from the accumulated millennia of gardening experience in these regions, but our own backyard can supply something they cannot.

Blue grama grass (*Bouteloua gracilis*)

Gold-flowered western sneezeweed (*Hymenoxys hoopesii*) and Rocky Mountain penstemon (*Penstemon strictus*) below bristlecone pines (*Pinus aristata*)

Great Sand Dunes, CO

The vast and primal topography of our deserts and grasslands have a powerful simplicity of style, and a complexity of composition that cannot be absorbed at seventy-five miles per hour. South Dakota's fabled Claude Barr spent a lifetime immersed in the study and promotion of the untapped riches of the Great Plains and the West. He captured his experience with eloquent style in his famous work, *Jewels of the Plains* (University of Minnesota Press, 1983):

**"Yesterday almost at dusk, neighbors brought their guests to see the garden. Although some white evening primroses were out, the large-flowered yellow kinds were at best just showing the promise of color between the rupturing calyx segments, a full hour beyond normal opening. Fifteen minutes later, when alone, I took another turn about the garden, to find many of the yellow ones displaying a dozen or more open suns—or moons if you like—though their color is a far more intimate tone than the most brilliant moon, and about them is an air of softness and generosity which dispenses a breathable atmosphere suitable to our earth. ... Of course, the joys of gardening are to be experienced on the road as well as in the garden. ... With good fortune, one may happen upon a long-sought and diminutive bright treasure, or a wide field of bloom, unexpected and unscheduled. ... The search for unusual forms of plants has given me skills in close observation and discrimination, and has lent a sense of purpose and zest to this best of all hobbies."**

Left to itself, our natural landscape presents a palette of sage and rust, tan, green and gold under a yawning dome of blue sky. Against this backdrop, our intoxicating sunlight ignites the blooms of Indian paintbrush (*Castilleja integra*) and blanket flower (*Gaillardia aristata*), and our blue skies are mirrored in the uplifted faces of blue flax. Frothy purple spikes of dotted gayfeather leap sun-drenched from their tawny beds of blue grama grass.

While the grand landscapes can draw us in, it is this richness of detail that can bind us more seamlessly to our surroundings. With a tangible sense of place, our homes and gardens and parkways need not jar so with the gentle curve of prairie or the fragrant sweep of ponderosa parkland. One needn't abandon horticulture to be responsible and attuned to landscape and climate. There is an untapped wealth yet to savor in the garden.

# TALE OF THE TUNDRA

By Mark Fusco

*The bristlecone pine forest at Mount Goliath is the defining reason for the M. Walter Pesman trail and the Dos Chappell Nature Center.*

Today the top of the M. Walter Pesman trail doesn't offer its usual view of Denver. Clouds envelope the foothills and plains, covering the horizon, prairie and city skyscrapers with a sea of billowy white. The white background is a perfect foil to the vast bristlecone pine (*Pinus aristata*) forest we see just below us at 12,000 feet. On these days above the clouds, the alpine and sub-alpine terrain seems even more removed from the Front Range, and as the sun shines brightly it is otherworldly.

Descending into the bristlecone pine forest one finds a mosaic of matting perennials and tufted crevice-dwelling alpines thriving amongst the boulders. The ancient pines above them refuse to be subordinated to any softened panoramic views. The twisted trunks and strips of bark manifest a thousand years of erosion that have turned their forms into sculpture. The bristlecone pine forest at Mount Goliath is the defining reason for the M. Walter Pesman trail and the Dos Chappell Nature Center.

## Life on the Tundra: Tenuous at Best

Denver has always been synonymous with the Rocky Mountains, and although the city sits on a vast high plain, a glance west reminds one that this is very much a mountain community. Arguably, the citizens of Denver have the best of both worlds: the short, mid and tall grass prairie remnants to the east and the dramatic Rocky Mountains to the west. Many who live here and many who visit are likely to become effusive when asked to describe these two worlds—places they go to when they leave the city in search of nature. They might describe the vistas, the serene grassy plains, the inspiring and challenging peaks, the plant life and the wildlife of each of those worlds.

Although words may not fail them, even those who often hike in the high country are unlikely to use the word tundra—unless it is being read from a guidebook. Only a few may be familiar with the word and fewer are likely to be able to define it. The tundra is the environment above treeline (about 11,500 feet in Colorado) in which a host of fragile and tiny plants and flowers grow in defiance of harsh elements: low temperatures, high winds, intense ultraviolet light, poor nutrient content in the soil and heavy snowfalls.

In the tundra, life is tenuous at best. Those who visit it can find beauty and inspiration in the struggle for life: in the diminutive alpines like the rosette-leaved rock jasmine (*Androsace chamaejasme*); the crevice gardens whose cracks burst with vibrant shades of tiny blooms; the burnished and gnarled trunks of thousand-year-old trees; and the ubiquitous rocks and boulders that make this life possible.

The sun is seen rising through a stand of bristlecone pines (*Pinus aristata*).

Bristlecone pine (*Pinus aristata*).

## From Rock Comes Life

Nothing is more indicative of the Rocky Mountains in general and of the tundra in particular than boulders and rocks. In fact, the abundance of boulders in the high country inspires many city homeowners to haul tons of rock into their gardens as "signature" pieces that provide symbolism and nostalgia of the high country.

The boulders that abound in the tundra are more than decorative. Without the decomposition of the igneous, metamorphic and sandstone rock that serves as the backbone of the Rocky Mountains, the soil on which the plants live would not exist. Here in the West, "soil" forms slowly from the erosion of rock and the decomposition of scant organic matter. After the soil was created, the plants slowly evolved and carved their individual niches out of what humans often regard as harsh conditions. Anthropomorphically speaking, the plants should not find much comfort in tundra conditions.

Plants, however, are opportunists, and in many situations tundra conditions reduce competition between plants and, therefore, give certain species an advantage. For example, plants like Rocky Mountain nailwort (*Paronychia pulvinata*), living within an alpine fellfield (a Scandinavian term for rock field), do not have to compete with grasses and other forbs largely because of the absence of soil. With little available soil and high winds, these plants have adapted by growing as low mats and utilizing a taproot. The mat catches bits of sand and soil, harvesting its own growing medium out of thin air.

Rocks, boulders and entire mountains come into play on the tundra. Many plants use the rocks, not just the soil they provide, to help them live and thrive within the weather conditions of the Rocky Mountains. These plants aren't just clinging to survival; they are reveling in their own success. A plant's dependence on rock can be as simple as its need for a well-drained, nutrient-deficient soil. Less subtle dependencies come in the form of protection from wind and ultraviolet light. The rocks and boulders can often keep nearby plants warm in the winter and cool in the summer. Plants exploit fissures and cracks in boulders as easy paths for roots to mine for water and the nutrients the water carries. As you can see, it is not at all far-fetched to say that many species of plants would probably not exist if it weren't for rocks, boulders and mountains. There is no place better than the Rocky Mountains to witness these plant-rock interactions.

> Many plants use the rocks, not just the soil they provide, to help them live and thrive within the weather conditions of the Rocky Mountains.

The M. Walter Pesman Trail showcases the most accessible stand of bristlecone pines (*Pinus aristata*) in Colorado.

## A Mountain Garden Not to Be Missed

Just a short drive from Denver (at the Idaho Springs exit on I-70), Mount Evans is by far the most accessible "fourteener" in Colorado. Visitors can drive on a paved road to the peak of this towering 14,264-foot mountain and enjoy the amazing vistas. As they travel up the winding steep road, they may stop at Summit Lake for a short walk before continuing on to the summit, from which they can catch glimpses of Mount of the Holy Cross or popular Gray's and Torrey's peaks. As fulfilling as that expedition is, the visit is hardly complete without a stop at an exceptional trail and an outstanding nature center just below the summit of Mount Goliath, a sub-peak and northern shoulder of Mount Evans. Mount Goliath, which rises to 12,216 feet above sea level, harbors two jewels: the M. Walter Pesman Trail and at the terminus of the Pesman Trail, Denver Botanic Gardens' satellite Alpine Rock Garden at the Dos Chappell Nature Center.

The M. Walter Pesman Trail showcases the most accessible stand of bristlecone pines (*Pinus aristata*) in Colorado. Within a mile of the trailhead, you will be in the middle of the second largest bristlecone pine forest in the state, with some trees as old as 1,600 years. The icing on this ancient cake consists of the alpine plant communities with their respective inhabitants occupying specialized niches or freely growing throughout the tundra. Six of the seven alpine plant communities are found along this trail or in the Alpine Rock Garden. Those six communities are: dry meadow; wet meadow; krummholz; fellfield; bristlecone pine forest; and crevice, talus and scree. Snowbed communities do not exist at either site.

A stand of windswept bristlecone pines (*Pinus aristata*).

Old man of the mountain (*Tetraneuris grandiflora*) sits in front of the Dos Chappell Nature Center.

The 1.5-mile trail begins at approximately 12,160 feet in the treeless tundra and traverses a fellfield dotted with prostrate pink-flowered moss campion (*Silene acaulis*), mounding Rocky Mountain nailwort (*Paronychia pulvinata*) with tiny chartreuse flowers, and (if you're lucky and aren't too proud to get down on your knees) you may have the chance to smell the blueberry-scented, aptly named alpine forget-me-not (*Eritrichium aretioides*). After a gradual ascent, the trail will give way to patches of meadow and rock crevice communities. In the meadow, impressive yellow sweeps of old man of the mountain (*Tetraneuris grandiflora*) display their prominent heads while the flower-haloed alpine spring beauty (*Claytonia megarhiza*) tuck themselves into the tight shady boulder crevices. Pretty soon you reach Mount Goliath peak (12,216 feet) and see the outline of the bristlecone pine forest in the distance. During the ensuing descent through a dry meadow community, you may notice a yellow flower with the moniker stemless four-nerve daisy (*Tetraneuris acaulis* var. *acaulis*).

Along the trail, dry meadow and rock crevice plant communities give way to the krummholz (German for "crooked wood"), windswept alpine regions close to treeline. Twisted bristlecone pines and Engelmann spruce (*Picea engelmannii*) cover the hillside below, displaying the gnarled and stunted character of carefully groomed bonsai. A continued descent through the krummholz leads you to the next alpine community, ancient bristlecone pine forest, and a glimpse into time. You may linger in admiration, surrounded by thousand-year-old trees. Follow the trail through a forest of subalpine fir (*Abies lasiocarpa*), bristlecone pine and Engelmann spruce and finish your hike at lower Goliath parking area and the Dos Chappell Nature Center. But your journey is far from over.

Sky pilot (*Polemonium viscosum*)

Alpine spring beauty (*Claytonia megarhiza*)

Gardening with altitude: *Cultivating a New Western Style*

Dos Chappell Nature Center stands behind purple fringe (*Phacelia sericea*)

*The soft rays of the sun shine on bristlecone pine (Pinus aristata).*

## Transformation to an Alpine Rock Garden

Since the early 1960s, Denver Botanic Gardens, which had been using the M. Walter Pesman trail to conduct tours, had an agreement with the U.S. Forest Service that the Gardens would do routine maintenance along the trail. Behind this agreement was M. Walter Pesman, a Denver Botanic Gardens board member for whom the trail was named.

By 1997, the lower end of the M. Walter Pesman Trail was unsightly, marred by several social trails and an undefined parking lot. Eventually, the Garden Club of Denver funded the construction of a garden to serve as a gateway to the lower trailhead; the plan was to reclaim the damaged parking area as a high-altitude rock garden. Ultimately, Denver Botanic Gardens and the U.S. Forest Service teamed up to build the garden. Panayoti Kelaidis, Director of Outreach at the Gardens, invited Zdenek Zvolanek, a rock garden designer from the Czech Republic, to come to Colorado and design this garden.

Zvolanek constructed the garden in just two weeks with the aid of U.S. Forest Service staff, Denver Botanic Gardens staff and volunteers. It was surprising and impressive how quickly and yet deliberately he pieced together boulders and rocks found at the site to construct the garden. When the alpine rock garden was completed, it featured a naturally fed stream and pond (a feature that nobody anticipated), small rock outcrops and meadow areas.

At the same time that the alpine satellite garden was being constructed, the Forest Service, with help from Volunteers for Outdoor Colorado (VOC), was also rebuilding the lower part of the M. Walter Pesman Trail. The newly defined trail eliminated the need for the braided social trails that descended through a large stand of willows near the new rock garden. As the Forest Service laid out the new trail, volunteers would carefully dig up plants and move them into the new rock garden. Shrubby cinquefoils (*Potentilla fruticosa*) were placed in the drier parts of the garden alongside the likes of purple fringe (*Phacelia sericea*), cutleaf daisy (*Erigeron compositus*) and Front Range beardtongue (*Penstemon virens*). In two weeks, the previous parking area was transformed into a naturalistic garden that looked like it belonged in the high mountain setting. Filled with native plants found on Mount Goliath, the garden has proven to be a successful reclamation. During the following three years, more native plants were added and the garden was slowly filled in. Along the stream and pond, white marsh marigold (*Caltha leptosepala*), elephant's heads (*Pedicularis groenlandica*) and star gentian (*Swertia perennis*) were planted. Grasses and sedges were added, which made the garden look more like the surrounding tundra; the new additions served as nurse plants and mulch for many of the colorful forbs.

Elephant's head (*Pedicularis groenlandica*)

## TIPS ON ADDING ROCK FEATURES TO YOUR GARDEN

When designing a rock feature in your home garden, be sure that you use rock that is in harmony with your house colors, with the neighborhood and with existing rock on your property. Local stone and a regional flavor are always the best policy.

Do not use rock of the same size. Vary your selections with a few large boulders, a range of midsize rock, and plenty of small rocks as well. Unless you are striving for a formal look, rocks should not be placed in regular patterns. Some rock should be touching; others can be placed with some large spaces and clusters.

Be sure all rock is firmly grounded, preferably so you can step on it without the rock budging. For many rocks this means they will be mostly buried.

Your rock feature should be attractive without any plants. Plants should not be used to cover your sins.

Remember that rock is heavy and potentially dangerous. Do not overtax your back and learn to obtain professional help if necessary.

Perhaps you can construct a scale model with pebbles of your rock design in a beer flat filled with sand. It's a great way to make mistakes cheaply and easily!

Bringing rocks into your garden is a great way of creating a sense of permanence and tying your garden into the landscape. Once they are installed, rocks are the lowest maintenance part of a landscape. Good luck!

The trail and paths around the garden were finished by VOC soon afterward, and the new rock garden served as a gateway to the lower section of the M. Walter Pesman Trail for the next four years. This small alpine garden generated even more interest in the special site among the partners (U.S. Forest Service, Denver Botanic Gardens, Garden Club of Denver and VOC). Dos Chappell, Director of VOC, lead the charge to build a nature center at the site and by 2003 construction was complete. The small alpine garden already found at the site served as inspiration for the landscaping around the nature center, and this landscaping evolved into the interpretive garden found there today.

Around the nature center, you may notice large boulders, skeleton pines and many of the plants you saw along the Pesman Trail. You've arrived at the Alpine Rock Garden, designed and constructed by Denver Botanic Gardens staff and volunteers. If you take a closer look, you will find that the garden is more than just a complement to the Dos Chappell Nature Center… it is part of it. Aesthetically, the garden serves to link the building to the natural area and the original alpine garden. Educationally, it is constructed to replicate and represent six different plant communities found on Mount Goliath, which are interpreted in the Dos Chappell Nature Center. As you examine the garden areas, you will encounter a crevice garden, cracks stuffed with mounds of sulfur-flowered James' buckwheat (*Eriogonum jamesii* var. *xanthum*) and bracted alumroot (*Huechera bracteata*) and skunk scented sky pilot (*Polemonium viscosum*), a fellfield full of grey blue cushion phlox (*Phlox pulvinata*), mats of white twinflower sandwort (*Minuartia obtusiloba*) and small mounds of moss campion (*Silene acaulis*). You can examine the climax community of the dry meadow grasses and sedges interspersed with alpine paintbrush (*Castilleja puberula*), white lollipops of American bistort (*Polygonum bistortoides*) and blue harebells (*Campanula rotundifolia*). A few steps beyond, you can see yellow and red paintbrushes (*Castilleja occidentalis* and *Castilleja rhexifolia*) next to a bevy of pink elephant's heads (*Pedicularis groenlandica*) in the wet meadow. In the near future, there will even be a bristlecone pine forest, interspersed with Jacob's ladder (*Polemonium pulcherrimum* ssp. *delicatum*) and giant red Indian paintbrush (*Castilleja miniata*), complete with a krummholz. At completion, you will be able to see all 257 species of plants growing on Mount Goliath at this single naturalistic garden site.

A short drive, incredible vistas, sweeps of wildflowers, one-thousand-year-old trees and North America's highest garden are just a few reasons to take this journey. Do come and see for yourself.

James' buckwheat (*Eriogonum jamesii* var. *xanthum*)

Rock Alpine Garden at Denver Botanic Gardens.

## ROCKS ON A PLAIN

The use of rocks throughout Denver Botanic Gardens is quite evident and serves to identify this garden with its natural surroundings, namely the Rocky Mountains. These same rocks also serve to link Denver Botanic Gardens to the high plains of Colorado, where many rock outcrops can be found. Places like Pawnee Buttes, Mesa de Maya and Comanche Grasslands feature rock formations as interesting and varied as one can discover throughout the mountainous areas of Colorado. Many of these formations also feature examples of juniper (*Juniperus* spp.), piñon (*Pinus edulis*) and limber pine (*P. flexilis*) remnants from a time when the Great Plains was filled with vast expanses of forests. It is no surprise that these small populations are growing among rock formations, which aided their survival.

It only seems natural to feature rocks in many of the gardens at Denver Botanic Gardens. Rocks and especially large boulders lend a natural beauty to gardens, anchor the garden to the land and give it a permanent feel. Aesthetically, they serve as a backdrop and companion to all varieties of plants. The variation in rock shape, size, texture, color and type can be almost as interesting as the plants themselves. Each type of rock, like all plants, has a story to tell. For example, granite from Mount Evans is very different from Pikes Peak granite, the latter having more pink coloration due to the abundance of feldspar whereas Mount Evans granite contains more gray and tan hues. Utilization of different types of rock within Denver Botanic Gardens gives each garden a sense of place and personality.

Rock soapwort (*Saponaria ocymoides* 'Alba') cascades through the Rock Alpine Garden.

TALE OF THE TUNDRA

Here, in
one spot,
the visitor can
catch vistas
in miniature of
distinct ecosystems
from a wide variety
of Colorado
elevations
and sites.

## STONE CONTAINERS: MAKE YOUR OWN ROCKS

The most novel use of rocks at Denver Botanic Gardens may be in Wildflower Treasures. This central flagstone plaza, which is based on the design of the trough garden at Royal Botanic Gardens, Edinburgh, is filled with 29 hypertufa troughs and surrounded by a rich diversity of plants from the dryland and mountainous West. (Hypertufa is an artificial stone made from various aggregates bonded together using Portland cement.) Each of the 29 containers consists of a miniature landscape featuring rocks, gravel and plants from specific localities in the state of Colorado. Here, in one spot, the visitor can catch vistas in miniature of distinct ecosystems from a wide variety of Colorado elevations and sites. Many troughs display rare and threatened plants.

Wildflower Treasures literally depicts the notion of a "sense of place." Plants native to the Great Plains and Rocky Mountains thrive in proximity to one another, giving visitors a capsule view of the diversity of western flora. Visitors can enjoy Wildflower Treasures for its impressive display of brilliant spring and early summer show of native wildflowers, as well as for its educational value.

Autumn sage (*Salvia greggii* Wild Thing™)

GARDENING WITH ALTITUDE: *Cultivating a New Western Style*

Troughs in Wildflower Treasures.

Tale Of The Tundra — Stone Containers: Make Your Own Rocks

Avery Peak twinpod (*Physaria alpina*)

Making troughs, if not glamorous, is rewarding. They are fun and fairly simple to create, and they add an aesthetic and functional addition to any garden. In the case of Wildflower Treasures, they form the backbone of the garden, much like the boulders of a rock garden. Creating a solid framework, the troughs contrast with the softness of mat-forming alpines while complementing spiny cacti. However, aesthetics are only a fraction of the purpose behind trough gardening.

The function of the troughs is of equal or greater importance to that of form and aesthetics. Most of the plants housed in the troughs of Wildflower Treasures would be lost in a traditional perennial border or cottage garden; the troughs provide a place where miniature native plants can thrive and patrons can view the collections.

Troughs also serve to enhance the cultural requirements necessary to grow these natives. Most of the alpine and dryland species living in Wildflower Treasures require well-drained soils. This condition is easily met by combining good topsoil, sand and a soil conditioner; peat moss is added to troughs that will be planted with alpines. For troughs that contain dryland plants or cacti, sand is substituted for peat moss. Proper drainage allows the lime from Portland cement to percolate through the soil to create a basic pH in which alpines and dryland natives thrive. The thickness of these containers ensures root protection from summer heat and a barrier from winter cold.

California fuschia (*Epilobium canum* ssp. *garrettii*) overlooks Wildflower Treasures.

Trough containers are best used for the most valuable and interesting small perennial plants that otherwise would get lost in the garden. For example, the Mosquito Range Trough, found in Wildflower Treasures, includes mountain avens (*Dryas octopetala*), with its shiny leaves and white daisy-like flowers, and the endemic Avery Peak twinpod (*Physaria alpina*). The plants are tucked among the same rock types in which they naturally grow. Adjacent to this trough is the Pikes Peak Trough, in which the luminous blooms of littleleaf alumroot (*Heuchera hallii*) grow beside the deep purple rock clematis (*Clematis columbiana* var. *tenuiloba*) planted between chunks of Pikes Peak granite. Perhaps the finest reward is watching these plants come alive in early spring. Genetically programmed to bloom within a short growing season, alpine plants seize the moment, and at the first sign of spring they put on a show of color, blooming several months earlier at Denver's 5,280-foot altitude than they do above treeline in the Rocky Mountains. Just a short distance away, one can find Colorado beardtongue (*Penstemon auriberbis*), *Penstemon versicolor* and roundleaf bladderpod (*L. ovalifolia* ssp. *ovalifolia*) living together happily in the Pueblo County Trough.

Butterfly milkweed (*Asclepias tuberosa*) in Wildflower Treasures.

GARDENING WITH ALTITUDE: *Cultivating a New Western Style*

Giant hyssop (*Agastache barberi*)

Fendler's aster (*Aster fendleri*)

The outer beds surrounding the plaza are filled with herbaceous perennials grouped according to the region from which they hail. North-south-east-west directions are used as an easy reference for visitors. For example, the eastern bed is filled with pink large beardtongue (*Penstemon grandiflorus*), purple gayfeather (*Liatris punctata*), bright orange butterfly milkweed (*Asclepias tuberosa*) and the blue false indigo (*Baptisia australis*). All of these Great Plains and tallgrass prairie perennials are perfectly suited to Colorado's dry climate and bloom reliably year after year. My favorite garden bed is probably the southern bed, which features plants from New Mexico, Arizona and southern Colorado. Two hyssops that stand out are sunset hyssop (*Agastache rupestris*) and giant hyssop (*Agastache barberi*). The former is a Plant Select winner with salmon-orange blooms; the latter has raspberry inflorescence. From the mint family, both hyssops attract hummingbirds and have a sweet, lemony scent. Sunset hyssop is somewhat more drought tolerant and a bit hardier, and all hyssops are excellent for any home garden. In Wildflower Treasures, these are interplanted with hot pink sage (*Salvia greggii* Wild Thing™) and red New Mexico figwort (*Scrophularia macrantha*). Hummingbirds love these plants!

The garden beds were not at all difficult to construct, and once the plants became established, maintenance has been a snap. When the beds were made, unamended topsoil was brought in and piled 6 inches to 1 foot higher than the surrounding sidewalks and flagstone plaza. The soil was mounded higher in the middle and sloped down to the flagstone grade, which ensures good drainage and keeps the plants from getting wet feet. After the plant installation was completed, a 1-inch to 2-inch layer of rock mulch was spread over the entire bed. The mulch keeps the soil cooler in the hot summer months and reduces cracking and frost heave in the winter. Mulch is an especially important component to any dryland garden. In Wildflower Treasures, generous amounts of pea gravel are used. This type of mulching is quite applicable to a home garden and is an excellent choice for a hot dry location in your yard (Who, living along Colorado's Front Range, doesn't have a spot like this?) and especially for a hell strip—that no-man's-land between the sidewalk and curb.

The lesson visitors can take away from this spot is that there is a place in every garden where a bit of the tundra and the Great Plains can find a home. Rocky Mountain plants, the rocks they grow among and native drought tolerant plants are becoming a defining feature of the many gardens in Denver Botanic Gardens.

## MAKE YOUR OWN TROUGH

The hypertufa troughs in Wildflower Treasures stimulate the curiosity of visitors, many of whom are seeing such containers for the first time. The troughs are unusual. They're gratifying to make, they give substance and character to the home garden, and you can make your own trough with these insider secrets!

**Hypertufa trough mix recipe:**
One part Portland cement
One part peat moss
One part perlite or vermiculite
Generous amount of nylon fiber mesh (about two handfuls per wheelbarrow)
Powdered concrete dye

Combine Portland cement, peat moss, perlite (or vermiculite) and fiber mesh in a wheelbarrow or any similarly sized container. Be sure to break up chunks of peat moss and fiber mesh. Mix all the dry ingredients and then add enough water to create the consistency of cookie dough. Add the dye until desired color is achieved. Be generous since the color will fade over time.

**Making the trough:**
First, start with a mold. Suitable molds include large plastic dishpans for rectangular troughs, baby baths for oval troughs and plastic terra cotta-colored planters for round troughs. Alternatively, you can build your own mold out of plywood. Be sure to drill a hole in the bottom of the mold to allow moisture to escape.

Hand-pack the hypertufa mixture onto the mold, blotting out excess moisture. Allow the trough to dry for at least one day. The hypertufa should be hard and dry enough that you cannot push your finger into the mixture, but soft enough so your fingernail can penetrate the surface. Gently remove the trough from the mold, then carefully rough up the outside of the trough (which rested against the mold) with a wire brush. After it's separated from the mold, let the trough dry for at least five days.

# THE ALLURE OF WATER

By Joe Tomocik

The ever-present mallard ducks glide easily and methodically from plant to plant, cleaning the leaves and satisfying their appetites as they go. Occasionally one disappears back-side up, searching for food from the pool bottom. The waterlilies are blooming profusely, radiating their brilliance for all to see. Clumps of marginals—cattails, rushes and grasses—create islands that mesh seamlessly with the multitude of waterlilies. Beyond the water garden's gazebo, pastel petals of awe-inspiring lotus lift skyward.

Admirers from across the pond and towering high-rise apartments reflect dramatically in the still water. "Mommy, look over there," gleefully exclaims a young child as she points to an especially bright and beautiful waterlily. "That is the best one of all!"

It is summertime and, to me, there is no better place to be than the Monet Garden horseshoe pool at Denver Botanic Gardens.

> From ancient times, water gardens have brought a sense of peace and tranquility to people in many cultures.

A tranquil moment at poolside.

An ever-present star: the mallard duck.

The Allure Of Water

In the summertime, there is no better place to be than the Monet Garden horseshoe pool at Denver Botanic Gardens.

## Water: Refreshing the Senses and the Soul

From ancient times, water gardens have brought a sense of peace and tranquility to people in many cultures. Water gardens were a feature of the legendary but perhaps fictitious Hanging Gardens of Babylon in the Middle East, and floating gardens near Mexico City had been a longstanding tradition by the time Spanish conquistadores arrived in the sixteenth century. Water gardens have always been a major focal point in Asian gardens, dating back to ancient Cathay.

Europe is equally famous for its many water gardens. Elaborate fountains were characteristic of Italian gardens, such as those in the Villa d'Este, which date from the sixteenth century and can still be enjoyed at Tivoli. In 1662, architect André Le Nôtre created the famous garden at Versailles, France, which contains a canal, hundreds of lakes, over one hundred fountains and bold statuary. Canals, large formal pools and cascades characterized early English gardens. In the nineteenth century, Joseph Paxton created the Emperor Fountain in Chatsworth (Suffolk, England) and successfully cultivated the first Victoria waterlily (*Victoria amazonica*) in 1849. A succession of important English gardens followed, starting with Longstock Gardens (west of London, in Hampshire) in 1870. Significant water gardens exist today at Kew Gardens (in London) and the Royal Horticultural Society Gardens in Wisley (Surrey). Stapeley Water Gardens (south of Nantwich) is probably the most impressive water gardening nursery in all of England.

The New World also has historic water gardens. In the United States, the Brooklyn Botanic Gardens, Longwood Gardens (Kennett Square, Pennsylvania) and the Missouri Botanical Garden (St. Louis) are esteemed water gardens. Those of Missouri and Longwood are especially well known for their marvelous displays of tropical waterlilies. Patrick Nutt of Longwood Gardens and Dr. George H. Pring of Missouri Botanic Gardens are famous for their success in hybridizing tropical waterlilies. As the name would suggest, Lotusland in Santa Barbara, California, boasts an elaborate display of lotus.

Photograph-Joe Tomocik

Glistening stigmatic fluid in this tropical waterlily's (*Nymphaea* 'Lindsey Woods') center tells us this is a first-day flower, ready for pollination.

## GEMS OF THE WATER GARDEN

Water alone can bring much to a garden: ever-changing, it captures light, reflections of the sun and clouds, and mirrored images of surrounding objects and those within the garden itself. For a true water garden, other elements are added to create a world of enchantment: jewel-colored lotus blooms, dazzling waterlilies, elegant large-leaved cannas and an array of striking foliage. Waterfowl change the images to ripples as they land, paddle and dive. Fountains and sculptures add movement, structure and form.

## THE LOTUS:
## JEWEL OF ANCIENT AND MODERN WATER GARDENS

For centuries, the regal lotus has arisen out of the mud, flowering in a blaze of glory. In time, the lotus disappears, only to return in a seemingly eternal renewal that has inspired humankind for millennia. The lotus was at one time thought to be in the same family as the waterlily. Recent taxonomic thought places it in a different family, *Nelumbonaceae*, in the genus *Nelumbo*.

History attests to the enduring importance of the lotus, both as an ornamental plant and a powerful symbol. The symbolism of the lotus has its roots in features of the landscapes of ancient cultures—Indian, Egyptian, Sumerian and even indigenous American. Leaves of the East Indian lotus (*Nelumbo nucifera*), which became naturalized in Egypt along the Nile, were found in the tomb of the great pharaoh Ramses II. That lotus and the blue Egyptian lotus (*Nymphaea caerulea*) are depicted on Egyptian fresco paintings, which show palace water gardens filled with lotus and other aquatics.

The East Indian lotus is also sacred in China, India, Tibet and Japan. In the practice of kudalini yoga, for example, total enlightenment is represented by a lotus with a thousand petals. In Japan, the East Indian lotus is respected as a symbol of life because all its parts can be eaten. It also signifies sincerity and nobility.

The hourglass-shaped lotus seed pod is a favorite in dried flower arrangements.

There is always something new, maybe even a bit bizzare, in the reflection pool. It's all part of the allure of water!

Containerized plants, waterlilies, lotus and reflections combine for an inviting scene.

## The Waterlily: Dazzling Color Afloat

Waterlilies also have fascinated people for millennia and, unlike lotus, may be either hardy or tropical. Waterlilies are in the family *Nymphaeaceae*, which include the so-called true waterlilies (*Nymphaea*), as well as *Victoria* waterlilies, spatterdocks (*Nuphar*) and other genera. Hardy waterlilies are native to Asia, Europe, and North and Central America. Tropical waterlilies, which may be day or night-blooming, come primarily from Central and South America, Australia and Africa.

## The Victorias: Floating Fragrance

Victoria waterlilies were discovered in South America in the early 19th century. They were named after then-reigning Queen Victoria of England by botanist John Lindley in 1837. Their cultivation in England frustrated enthusiasts for years until 1849, when *Victoria amazonica* not only survived but also bloomed at Chatsworth, the estate of the Duke of Devonshire.

## The Marginals: More Colors, Shapes and Forms

"Marginal" is a rather generic term, which I use to illustrate aquatic plants that are not waterlilies or lotus. The plants can be hardy or tropical, and of various forms and colors. They are very effective when displayed by themselves, with other marginals or with waterlilies. Examples of easy and effective marginals used in our displays include the bold foliaged hardy canna (*Thalia dealbata*), upright cattails (*Typha angustifolia, T. latifolia* and *T. laxmannii*) and aromatic sweet flag (*Acorus calamus*). An outstanding marginal used frequently is prairie cordgrass (*Spartina pectinata*), which grows in or out of the water to a height of four feet when planted in a five-gallon container. It turns a golden brown in late summer and is easily propagated by seed or division. One of the drawbacks of prairie cordgrass is its tendency to be invasive.

A bee pollinates this exotic tropical waterlily, which flowers abundantly throughout the summer

## CREATING A WATER GARDEN

Do you have an interest in water gardening? What are you waiting for? The days of restricting water gardens to botanic gardens, parks and formal estates are over. Of course, one needs to do some research before digging up the lawn. But water gardening is easy and the challenges are stimulating. Get a container, some aquatic plants and begin your container water garden today.

Information about water gardening is available in many excellent publications at the Gardens' own Helen Fowler Library. You can also pick up tips on water gardening practices by joining the Colorado Water Gardening Society. (See the reference list at the end of this book for print recommendations and Web sites.)

After you have created your garden, look forward to algae because it is likely to occur. During the growing season, we combat algae with a weekly application of a multistrain bacteria that removes the nutrients that algae need to thrive from the water.

Use floating plants. Aerate with a pump and fountain. Waterlilies need relatively quiet water. Marginals such as cattails (*Typha* spp.) and prairie cordgrass (*Spartina pectinata*) or sweet flag (*Acorus calamus*) can tolerate faster moving water.

Incorporate fish, statuary, benches, lights and container gardens. Don't be limited by designs you see at Denver Botanic Gardens. Let your imagination go. Your water garden doesn't have to be perfect; be an artist, be an innovator. Share your enthusiasm, and most importantly have fun!

Since the
summer of 1973,
visitors to Denver
Botanic Gardens
have enjoyed
an ingeniously
designed waterway
as a connecting
link for
the flourishing
gardens…

## DENVER'S DELIGHTFUL WATERWAY

In Colorado's semi-arid climate, water is particularly refreshing to the eye, ear and spirit. Since the summer of 1973, visitors to Denver Botanic Gardens have enjoyed an ingeniously designed waterway as a connecting link for the flourishing gardens framed by snow-capped peaks. Throughout the Gardens, the abundance of water allows for numerous grand opportunities to display a multitude of exciting aquatic plants from as far north as Alaska to as far south as South America and Africa.

Water enters the garden from a large fountain just west of the Romantic Gardens, situated in the southeastern corner of the Gardens. From here the water flows through a series of large and small pools and ponds, streams and canals. The water surges, churns, spills and drips. The musical sounds are ever present, but since most people are visually oriented, these sounds often go unnoticed. To hear them, it helps to pause, be still and listen carefully. Some visitors hear one water sound in one ear and a different sound in the other.

After it circulates throughout the Gardens, the water is pumped underground from the Cactus and Succulent House back to the fountain at the beginning of the waterway.

This extremely hardy and lovely waterlily (*Nymphaea* 'Denver's Delight') thrives in the Gardens' pool.
It was found growing in Denver's Berkeley Park.

## ROMANTIC GARDENS POOL

The water's route begins at the circular Romantic Gardens pool, which is well suited for a casual mix of hardy and tropical waterlilies with a centerpiece of lotus. When properly designed, the plants line up perfectly with the large fountain as one looks west from the east end of the turf area adjacent to the pool. The combination of hardy waterlilies, tropical waterlilies and lotus provide a flowering period from June into September. The hardies begin flowering in May/June, followed by the lotus and the tropicals in July. All bloom into September.

The stately and mystical lotus, which grows in the Romantic Gardens pool and throughout the other water gardens, is a favorite of visitors. There are only two species of lotus: the previously mentioned East Indian lotus (*Nelumbo nucifera*), which is native to India and China; and the American lotus (*N. lutea*), which is native to North America only. Many lotus varieties and hybrids have been developed by avid propagators.

Lotus are planted in late April or early May. Firm, healthy tubers are gently pushed into containers measuring 7 inches deep by 24 inches wide. Adjustments are made so that 4 or 5 inches of water cover the container. Lotus usually flower the first year. Warm temperatures and full sun are important factors in producing blooms. In addition, it is critical at planting time to avoid breaking the growing points, which are very brittle. Broken points can result in failure to bloom.

The best performing lotus at Denver Botanic Gardens is *Nelumbo nucifera* 'Mrs. Perry D. Slocum', which was hybridized by the late Perry D. Slocum, prolific nurseryman, hybridizer, photographer and author. This selection flowers consistently; the blooms are yellow the first day, pink and yellow the second day and pink the third.

The so-called teacup lotus, about which much has been written, is a small variety rumored to flower in teacup-sized containers. Although this is a bit of an exaggeration, we have been able to keep one very small hybrid (thanks to volunteer par excellence John Bayard), *N.* 'Jade Bowl', which will do well and flower in a 9-inch-wide container or possibly one a bit smaller. Teacup lotus has value as an ornamental because its oval horizontal leaves rise above the pot.

Perry's Giant Sunburst lotus (*Nelumbo* 'Perry's Giant Sunburst'), one of the many outstanding introductions of legendary Perry D. Slocum.

> Rising from the mud, the regal lotus captures the depth of the soul.

The lotus holds the record for longevity of viable seed of any plant. In 1951, viable seeds of the variety 'Ohga Hasu', discovered in a bog near Tokyo, were proven to be 2,000 years old. Two seeds germinated, and the plant is now cultivated throughout the world, including at Denver Botanic Gardens—where it is grown from seed.

The large lotus at Denver Botanic Gardens are overwintered by insulating them with fallen leaves or pine needles in plastic garbage bags. The lotus are carefully stacked high in a concrete bin on the west side of the greenhouses and covered by the bags. This keeps them from drying out or freezing. The smaller varieties are kept in a cold greenhouse at winter temperatures maintained at 40 degrees F.

There are two risks to successfully growing lotus in the Gardens and in the Denver area. The first are the damaging hailstorms that are not uncommon in the summer and, in fact, can be expected every three to five years. Lotus are slow to recover from hail as the leaves are not numerous and do not replenish quickly. Another hazard occurs each spring, when to the dismay of all, as if being drawn in by magnets, Canada geese return, seemingly with the sole object of feeding on the lotus. On more than one occasion, lotus tubers have been found, soon after being planted, floating in the water mutilated! Although we use bricks to secure the tubers and wire baskets are placed over the containers, the geese still find a way to get at them. Eventually, however, the geese leave the area in early summer. We now place wire cages with smaller diameters over the lotus containers, which protects the newly planted tubers.

Visitors who carefully observe the Romantic Gardens pool may notice the black-colored water. Here and there in the main waterway a non-chemical (and thus nonpolluting) colorant is applied throughout the summer. The results are deeper reflections and more contrast between the water and plants.

Bi-colored waterlily (*Nymphaea* 'Mary').

Photograph-Joe Tomocik

GARDENING WITH ALTITUDE: *Cultivating a New Western Style*

The Romantic Gardens' pool showcases hardy and tropical waterlilies and lotus favorite *Nelumbo nucifera* 'Mrs. Perry D., Slocum'.

The pure white flower of this *Victoria cruziana* opened the previous night; a new leaf prepares to unfurl.

## Victoria Pool

From the Romantic Gardens pool, the water flows by way of the large fountain, filling the large L-shaped Victoria pool, which is ideal for displaying hardy and tropical waterlilies as well as the Victoria waterlily, which has only two species. *Victoria amazonica* and *V. cruziana* are native to the Amazon basin of South America. In North America, the plant first flowered in cultivation near Philadelphia in 1851 and at the Missouri Botanical Garden in 1884. In Denver, the Gardens' superlative Victoria display can be attributed in a large way to the nearby Victoria Conservancy at the home of Trey and Nancy Styler of Greenwood Village. With their help, a record-breaking 20 Victorias were displayed at the Gardens in 2001.

Typically, *V. cruziana* and *V.* 'Longwood Hybrid' (hybridized by Patrick Nutt, Longwood's legendary horticulturist and one of my early and favorite teachers) are planted in containers measuring 24 inches wide by 9 inches deep in mid-June, a full 7 to 10 days earlier than they did 20 years ago because the plants are now much larger. Their huge showy white flowers open at sunset and stay open in Denver until midday of the next day. (In other locations, they close at sunrise.) The flower opens red on the subsequent night, closing and ending its blooming cycle the following day. After a day of rest, another flower opens on the same plant. Especially on the first night of flowering, Victoria flowers emit a strong fruity fragrance that can be experienced from 50 feet away or more if there is a breeze.

The Victorias, a major attraction in late summer, flower well into September. Fairyland-like leaves up to five feet across with three-inch upturned edges (higher on *V. cruziana*) stop visitors in their tracks. The leaves of *V. cruziana* are green and those of *V.* 'Longwood Hybrid' are red. A breeze causes the leaves to gently sway back and forth. The rib network on the leaf undersides provide support and have inspired the design of major structures including the Crystal Palace in London, built for the Great Exhibition of 1851. Although it is common to see pictures of children standing on the leaves, these photos are usually the result of a photographer's trick: camouflaged support has been placed under the plant.

Growing Victorias in Denver can be challenging. Because of the cool nights, water temperatures are certainly cooler than optimum. As already noted, hail quickly destroys the leaves, which grow back slowly. Midge larvae can defoliate leaves on stressed plants. It helps to begin with healthy plants and refrain from adding make-up water (which comes in at a much lower temperature) unless absolutely necessary. Victorias are fed with fertilizer tablets each week. Because the plants are too large to bring inside for the winter, they are allowed to die off naturally in October.

From a design standpoint, the Victorias are so dramatic that it is quite a challenge to divert attention from them. It is best to simply flaunt them. Many visitors note the oddity of viewing the eloquent, gigantic exotic Victorias in midsummer against a backdrop of 14,000-foot snow-capped peaks in semiarid Denver, which is dominated with native plantings. It is part of the fun and certainly within the scope of a major botanic garden to create and successfully cultivate such inspiring displays.

Besides Victorias, choice tropical marginals in the Victoria pool include the large and stately papyrus (*Cyperus papyrus*), umbrella plant (*C. alternifolius*) and tufted dwarf papyrus (*C. haspan*).

Hardy waterlilies perform marvelously here, flowering earlier in the summer. Tailormade for this pool are the day- and night-blooming tropical waterlilies (*Nymphaea* spp. and cvs.). The tropical waterlilies are dynamic with wonderfully fragrant flowers rising above the water, opening and closing for three or four days or nights. They are planted in 5- to 7-gallon containers by about June 10 and are fertilized every three weeks. Unlike the hardy waterlilies, the tropicals can be blue or purple. Most of the species tropicals (*Nymphaea caerulea*, *N. capensis* and *N. lotus*) are from Africa.

The 'star waterlilies', which work really well in this pool, are large – up to 10 feet across for the spread of the plant. The flowers stand twelve inches or more out of the water on stout peduncles. This characteristic comes from the species *N. gracilis* of Mexico. *N.* 'Rhonda Kay', a purple selection, which often sports eight or more flowers at a time, is one of the best-performing tropical day-flowering varieties. It was hybridized by Ken Landon, of San Angelo, Texas.

## Reflection Pool

By way of a narrow channel, the water flows into the reflection pool. The marble statuary by Frank Swanson titled Reflection, which characterizes this pool, adds another dimension to the design. For centuries, statuary and sculptures have been integrated into water gardens because they provide a focal point.

The water in this pool moves a bit too fast for waterlilies. This pool is a fine place to display more lotus (*Nelumbo* cvs.) and marginals, including the colorful water canna (*Canna* cvs.). Favorites include the yellow *C.* 'Ra', pink *C.* 'Erebus', red *C.* 'Endeavour' and dark foliaged *C.* 'Australia'. Water canna are extremely effective aquatics capable of blooming year-round if brought inside at the end of summer.

The next pool, on the fringe of the exquisite Rose Garden, is rectangular and suitable for displaying marginals and waterlilies. The water then spills gently into additional rectangular pools—all of which are great for marginals, but not for waterlilies as the water moves too fast. These pools are also excellent without aquatics. It is not necessary to have plants in all the pools.

The water then churns pleasantly through another channel, filling the Sacred Earth pool, which has a display of hardy native marginals.

Upright foliage of sweet flag (*Acorus calamus*), an aromatic and easy-to-care-for hardy marginal, adds interest in one of the many Gardens' side pools.

The Allure Of Water

## Monet Garden's Horseshoe Pool

Large numbers of hardy waterlily *Nymphaea* are displayed in the Monet Garden's horseshoe pool, with major support from tropical waterlilies, lotus (*Nelumbo*) and Victoria waterlilies (*Victoria cruziana* and *V.* 'Longwood Hybrid').

The hardy waterlilies are divided, repotted and moved to the pools starting in April. They are fertilized every three weeks and their leaves are cleaned meticulously every week by volunteers through the summer. Flowering is usually in full force in June and continues into mid-September. The hardy waterlilies, like the tropical variety, produce flowers for three to four days that open in the morning and close in the afternoon. The flowers, extending as much as six inches across, rest on the water's surface. Large plants measure six to eight feet across. The miniature *Nymphaea* 'Pygmaea Helvola' has a plant diameter of 18 inches and sports precious two-inch flowers.

The creation of new hybrid waterlilies out of naturally occurring existing species is an irresistible challenge to water gardeners. The challenge is to create new colored, longer blooming, more vigorous and better flowering plants. Most of the hardies in the Gardens' collection are hybrids, and serious local water gardeners know them well. Important North American species include *Nymphaea odorata*, *N. tetragona* and *N. mexicana*.

The waterlilies of Monet's famous gardens were hybrids created by Joseph Bory Latour-Marliac. Some of these varieties are still considered to be among the best. Favorites in our collection include the colossal white *N.* 'Virginalis', tiny *N.* 'Indiana', deep red *N.* 'Escarboucle' and pastel pink *N.* 'Amabilis'. The exponential increased interest in water gardening over the past two decades or so (since the founding of the Colorado Water Gardening Society) has resulted in the introduction of a large group of new and exciting waterlilies. Specifically, the abundance of quality new introductions by Perry D. Slocum and Dr. Kirk Strawn have elevated them to a status second to none. Other important hybridizers include Kenneth Landon, Charles Winch, Patrick Nutt and Bruce and Brad McLane.

## Beyond Monet

The audience is lunching at the Monet Deck Café under the shade of the hackberry trees (*Celtis occidentalis*). The stage is the Monet Garden's horseshoe pond. The stars are the multitude of waterlilies and aquatic plants, mallard ducks, damsel flies and shimmering reflections. Surrounding the pond are such innovative gardens as Wildflower Treasures, the Drop Dead Red Border and the Gazebo, which set off the pond to perfection. The water crashes from the large pond moving over the falls through a short stream into the Japanese Garden pond.

Again the water moves through a short stream into the Gates Montane Garden pond, in which Gardens' curator Dan Johnson has created a marvelous planting of native aquatic prairie cordgrass (*Spartina pectinata*), common arrowhead (*Sagittaria latifolia*) and Rocky Mountain iris (*Iris missouriensis*) a native to Colorado. At this quiet terminus of the water's flow, tall reflections of the montane garden across the pool recall a tranquil lake at high altitude.

Aquatic marginal prairie cordgrass (*Spartina pectinata*) cradles waterlily *Nymphaea* 'Albert Greenberg'.

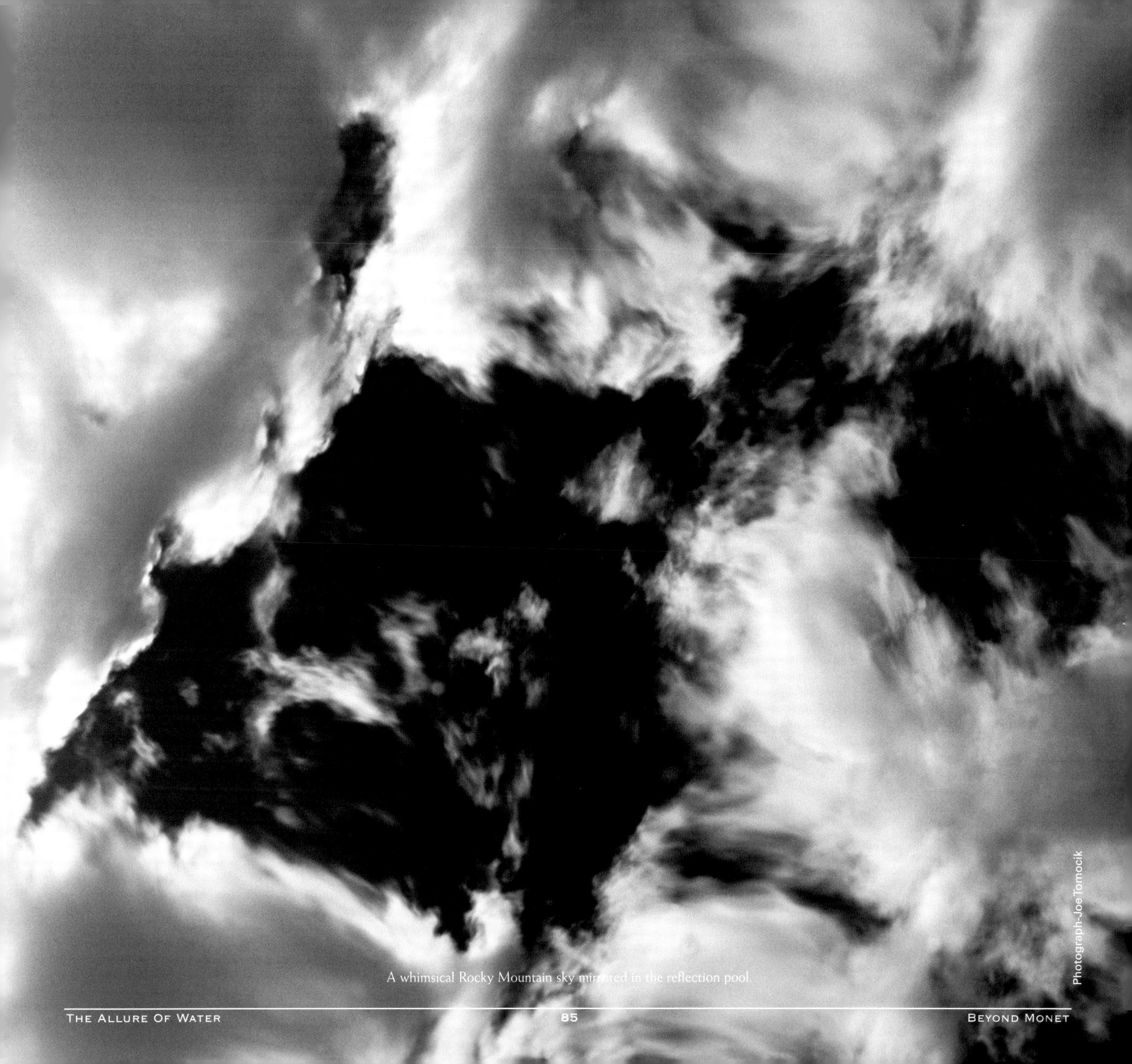

A whimsical Rocky Mountain sky mirrored in the reflection pool.

THE ALLURE OF WATER — BEYOND MONET

Photograph-Joe Tomocik

*Bright-colored cannas provide excitement throughout the summer.*

## WATER BY DESIGN

Aquatic plants and water are so potent one has to work hard to create an ineffective design. The range of designs is infinite as the themes change each year. The display in summer 2004 was designed around Chapungu, the Zimbabwean sculpture display; it was further enhanced as staff member Jonathan Knox, with African drum in hand, recounted stories in support of the sculptures as he walked around the pools with visitors. The theme of Monet's gardens and paintings was the basis for the 2005 design, incorporating the aforementioned hybrids.

Potted plants are moved into position to bring each year's story alive. Groups of waterlilies are interspersed with islands composed of marginals and open water. Effort is made to avoid regularity and sharp angles. The trick is to combine serenity with excitement.

The surrounding high-rise apartments are very much part of the scene, although they can be blocked out by changing the viewing position. The open water allows for dramatic reflections. Combining the many hardy and tropical waterlilies allows for a progression of color and maturity. Waterlilies of a wide color spectrum present an exciting brilliance. The mallard ducks moving easily (and at times frolicking) through the pools create spontaneous effects. Surrounding container gardens, strategically positioned and expertly designed and maintained, complete the design.

Although many visitors want to know the names of plants, labeling is a bit of a design challenge because it interferes with the views of the plants and the integrity of the design. We compromise by limiting labels to selected areas, which allows for more pristine plant views for artists and photographers.

Of course, design would be nothing without the see-er, the all-important Gardens' visitors. While horticulture is a science, it is also an art — and art requires an audience.

> Waterlilies of a wide color spectrum present an exciting brilliance.

Storied Colorado Water Garden Society volunteer Doris Freestone trims waterlilies in the Victoria pool.

## DENVER BOTANIC GARDENS: A FORCE FOR WATER

The beginning of a new age for water gardening in modern times arrived relatively recently. The world's first water gardening society was founded on February 13, 1983, when the Colorado Water Gardening Society (CWGS) was created in a Denver Botanic Gardens' classroom. Soon after, the International Waterlily and Water Gardening Society (IWGS) was created. Water gardening has grown at a rapid pace ever since, gaining an enthusiastic following worldwide.

Denver Botanic Gardens has remained a main force in this movement through programs such as indoor aquatic displays, waterlily trials (which introduce new waterlily hybrids) and the captivating outdoor Fly Trap Feast display (which demonstrates innovative use of container water gardens). The summer displays at the Gardens, which include more than 400 waterlilies and 1,000 plants, focus attention on the enduring power of water gardens, especially in a steppe climate such as ours. No one has challenged these displays as being the largest of any botanic garden.

The volunteer contribution of the CWGS in support of our water gardens is extraordinary. Every spring, members assist in putting our display together; in the fall they dismantle it. Their cooperation, energy and skill are paramount in the success of our Gardens. The volunteers also play an important part in providing water gardening education to Denver and the surrounding community. Every year, CWGS volunteers contribute 1,400 volunteer hours. John and Mary Mirgon, early volunteers and leaders (along with myself), have been awarded Hall of Fame awards by the IWGS for outstanding contributions.

The Monet Water Garden at Denver Botanic Gardens.

Hardy waterlily *Nymphaea* 'Indiana'

Photograph-Joe Tomocik

## PROTECTING THE GARDENS: CONSERVATION AND ECOLOGY

As horticulturists in a botanic garden, we are stewards of the environment. Like other ecosystems, wetlands are complex, delicate and precious.

While we are generating wonderful and inspiring gardens, we must not lose sight of the value of all plants and conservation. We remember that the early Egyptians made paper from papyrus (*Cyperus papyrus*); we are aware that sundew (*Drosera* spp.) are being tested for potential in fighting cancer; we know that Indians ate the roots of the spatterdock (*Nuphar lutea*) and that lotus roots, leaves and seeds are edible. Goldfish fall prey to the black-knighted heron; Venus flytraps (*Dionaea muscipula*) eat and digest dragonflies. Every plant, insect and animal is connected in an amazing web of life. A seemingly small change can ripple through an entire spectrum and instigate catastrophic damage.

By being aware of conventions and abiding by various agreements, we "water" our own gardens. The Convention on International Trade in Endangered Species of Wild Fauna and Flora (known as CITES) is an international agreement to which countries adhere voluntarily; the aim of CITES is to ensure that international trade in specimens of wild animals and plants does not threaten their survival. Not one species protected by CITES has become extinct as a result of trade since the convention entered into force. Plants protected by CITES include the Venus fly trap and pitcher plants (*Sarracenia oreophila*, *S. rubra*, *S. rubra* ssp. *alabamensis* and *S. rubra* ssp. *jonesii*). Reported to be threatened in their native Africa are papyrus (*Cyperus papyrus*) and the blue Egyptian lotus (*Nymphaea caerulea*).

Many aquatics propagate exponentially and are often capable of becoming serious pests when plants are removed from their natural environment. The U.S. Animal and Plant Health Inspection Service (APHIS) has the major function of controlling noxious weeds. After a noxious weed is added to the published list, it is unlawful for nurseries to possess and to sell them. Included in this list are the floating aquatics *Azolla pinnata* and *Salvinia molesta*. Each U.S. state has its own lists of weeds that are considered to be noxious in that particular state. For example, loosestrife (*Lythrum salicaria*) is considered to be a noxious weed in Colorado (as well as 29 other states), but is not considered a weed at all in some other states.

Integrated Pest Management (IPM), which employs the most environmentally safe techniques in controlling pests, is used throughout the Gardens, including the water garden. The cultivation of healthy plants using recommended practices pays huge dividends. Seriously infected and diseased plants are discarded.

As stewards of the environment, we must do our best to ensure that the web of life remains intact. Facing that challenge every day, we work to the highest standard throughout the Gardens. The water garden, an artistic fusion of water and plants, two entities of the natural world on which all life depends, is a potent reminder of that web. As we contemplate the beauty of water gardens, we respond wholeheartedly to its message to us.

Waterlily *Nymphaea* 'Devonshire'

# THE GARDENS UNDER GLASS

By Nick Snakenberg

The tropics . . . The word may conjure up a host of images: pristine white-sand beaches surrounded by an idyllic island landscape, dense vegetation in impenetrable steamy jungles, gigantic and wildly colored flowers or exotic wildlife in all shapes and sizes. We form these images from our notions of paradise, from images we see in the movies or on television, and even from travel advertisements urging us to escape our daily routines to experience the romance and excitement of far away lands. But what do most of us really know of the tropics and of the great importance that tropical plants play in our lives?

After we learn something about the tropics and tropical plants, we may be even more enchanted and tempted to make a personal visit. The intoxicating smell of our morning coffee, the exquisite bamboo floor in an entryway, or the relief we get from an anti-inflammatory medication are daily reminders of the importance of tropical ecosystems and may inspire a new vision of these rich lands.

## A Strange Mix: Tropical Plants and Colorado

Denver Botanic Gardens has a reputation for growing and displaying unique and unusual plants from around the world. But one might well wonder why a conservatory was built in semiarid Colorado for the explicit purpose of housing a large collection of tropical plants. In our dry climate, rainforest plants may seem out of place, but the Gardens' tropical plant collections not only provide a striking contrast to our native flora but also give visitors a larger appreciation of the diversity of plant life on earth and the role that these plants play in our everyday lives.

For me, one of the most enjoyable aspects of working at a botanic garden is the huge diversity of plant life I get to see and work with every day. I've been lucky to visit many parts of the world and to see a wide range of plant communities, but outside of a botanic garden there are few places on earth where you can see such plant diversity during a leisurely afternoon stroll.

*Dendrobium lindleyi*

Since its dedication in 1966, the Boettcher Tropical Conservatory has become a Denver landmark.

> Although most people think of the tropics as densely vegetated and steamy jungles, there are actually many varied ecosystems within these latitudinal boundaries.

## Tropical Rainforests: A Variety of Ecosystems

Our journey to tropical rainforests begins with a geographical definition. The tropics can be broadly defined as the portion of the earth's surface that falls between the Tropic of Cancer (23.5 degrees north latitude) and the Tropic of Capricorn (23.5 degrees south latitude). Although most people think of the tropics as densely vegetated and steamy jungles, there are actually many varied ecosystems within these latitudinal boundaries. Not only are there densely vegetated rainforests, but also frozen mountaintops, arid deserts, seasonally dry forests and vast grasslands. Rainfall and temperature are what set the rainforest apart. Tropical rainforests typically receive 80 to 400 inches of precipitation annually and do not experience a marked wet and dry season. Temperature remains remarkably constant throughout the year with a mean temperature falling somewhere between 70 and 85 degrees F.

At the highest elevation of a tropical rainforest, the temperature is somewhat cooler. You have now entered the cool, moist environment of a tropical upland rainforest, also known as a cloud forest. As the warm lowland rainforest air travels upslope to higher altitudes, the air is cooled and eventually condenses into clouds. While annual precipitation is similar to the lowland forests, average temperatures drop to as low as 65 degrees F. These cloud forest ecosystems normally occur at altitudes between 3,000 and 10,000 feet and are home to a wide range of plant and animal species uniquely adapted to the cool, moist and often low light conditions.

The Boettcher Tropical Conservatory provides a dramatic backdrop to many of the outdoor plantings at Denver Botanic Gardens.

Gardening with altitude: *Cultivating a New Western Style*

Visitors enjoy the lush and varied plantings inside the Boettcher Tropical Conservatory.

Red powderpuff (*Calliandra haematocephala*)

## Gifts from Tropical Forests

Three major tropical rainforest ecosystems exist in the world: the Congo Basin in Africa; the Malay Archipelago, which includes parts of Australia and Asia; and the Amazon Basin in South America. Within these tropical rainforests grow a great variety of plants that produce an astounding array of products used in all facets of our lives. Everything from food to fiber, lumber and medicines, and even ingredients for many cosmetics can be harvested from the tropical rainforests of the world. Many culinary staples are produced in the tropics, and the Boettcher Tropical Conservatory at Denver Botanic Gardens holds many examples of plants with important economic impacts on local and international economies.

From an aesthetic perspective, any list of favorite tropical plants is likely to include those from a wide variety of locales. Who can resist the spidery iridescent flowers of the red powderpuff (*Calliandra haematocephala*) from South America or the clear azure flowers of the blue butterfly bush (*Clerodendrum ugandense*) from Africa? Adults and children alike enjoy the prehistoric cycads such as the queen sago (*Cycas circinalis*) from India and the Mexican cycad (*Dioon spinulosum*). Looking toward the sky, visitors notice the wonderful architecture of the ant feeder tree (*Cecropia peltata*) from Jamaica and the triangle palm (*Dypsis decaryi*) of Madagascar. What a treat to visit so many corners of the world in only one trip to the Gardens!

## Coffee, Chocolate, Vanilla—and Panama Hats

The products of tropical rainforests are truly a treat to all the senses. More than 100 million coffee drinkers in the United States spend billions of dollars on a beverage brewed from the roasted fruits of *Coffea arabica* and *Coffea canephora*. Native to Africa and Asia, the plant from which coffee is made is now grown in tropical regions around the world in order to satisfy a huge global market.

Chocolate lovers follow close behind coffee fans. They consume mountains of candies, cakes, desserts and drinks made of their favorite flavoring; they owe great thanks to the chocolate tree (*Theobroma cacao*), which is native to Central and South America, although today more than seventy percent of the world's supply of cacao is produced in Africa.

A great divide separates chocolate fans from those who favor the "other" flavor: vanilla. Vanilla beans are actually fermented seedpods of the vanilla orchid (*Vanilla planifolia*), which is native to Mexico. Production of this popular flavoring has spread around the world.

Hawaii once produced and processed the majority of the world's pineapple (*Ananas comosus*), but rising costs have driven production to other countries including Brazil, Mexico, Malaysia and the Philippines. Visitors to the Boettcher Tropical Conservatory can see plants that produce many other tropical fruits and spices, including papaya (*Carica papaya*), guava (*Psidium guajava*), black pepper (*Piper nigrum*) and banana (*Musa* cvs.).

Pineapple (*Ananas comosus*)

The gifts that tropical forests offer us are not confined to those we put in our mouths. The plants in these rich forests are also an important source of many fibers. In Ecuador and other parts of South America, young leaves of the Panama hat plant (*Carludovica palmata*) are split into thin straps and woven together to make durable hats that have been worn since the 16th century. The hats originated in Incan culture and became known as Panama hats when workers on the Panama Canal used them for protection from the unrelenting heat and sun. In the Philippines, fibers from pineapple leaves are used to produce a delicate and expensive fabric known as piña cloth, which has been used for centuries for such luxury items as kimonos, handkerchiefs and table linens. Spanish moss (*Tillandsia usneoides*) has been used in upholstery and for stuffing automobile seat cushions.

For centuries, wood has been an important commodity for humans. It is essential as a fuel and also for shelter and furnishings. Many tropical woods are in high demand, including teak, mahogany and rattan. In the Boettcher Tropical Conservatory, you can see a number of plants used for building materials including balsa (*Ochroma pyramidale*), bamboo (*Bambusa* spp.) and mountain-grape (*Coccoloba pubescens*).

Tropical plants are also a source of many cosmetic agents. Those of us who use moisturizing products may be interested to learn that the oils from many palm seeds, which grow in the crown of the plant, are used as moisturizers in soaps and shampoos, and can also be used for culinary purposes. Essential oils from the champa tree (*Michelia champaca*) are used in fragrances and in lotions to soothe dry skin. Many people are familiar with patchouli (*Pogostemon cablin*), whose oils are used in fragrances and for aromatherapy.

## What the Doctor May Order

Tropical plants may go far beyond simply being sources of treats for our tastebuds, for fibers and building materials, and for cosmetics. Much work is being done to uncover the vast potential for new drugs and therapies originating in tropical forests. Researchers are aware that indigenous tribes have used many plants for medicinal purposes for hundreds of years. In the Amazon rainforests, whitewood (*Tabebuia* ssp.) has long been used as an herbal remedy for colds, flu, psoriasis and fungal infections by native people. In Asia, roots of Indian saffron (*Curcuma longa*) are used not only in cooking but also as an anti-inflammatory balm. With so many plants to be discovered, there are sure to be new remedies as well. We have only begun to realize the importance of tropical plants in medicine.

Papaya (*Carica papaya*)

# A TOUR OF DENVER'S TROPICAL COLLECTIONS

The plantings within the Boettcher Tropical Conservatory are designed to showcase plant species found in lowland tropical rainforests and also include cultivated varieties chosen for their exceptional form or color. With hundreds of thousands of tropical plants in the world, it would be impossible to collect, grow and display them all. With limited space, every botanic garden must realistically evaluate the facilities it has and what plant groups or families would best serve the institution's goals and needs. While the Gardens' tropical displays encompass a wide range of plant families, over the years several have obtained prominence in our collections.

## Epiphytes: Life on Top of Life

Many of the Gardens' earliest plant accessions are from a group known as epiphytes, which are plants that live upon other plants, using them as a means of support. Unlike parasites, epiphytes derive no nourishment from their hosts, but take advantage of increased light and nutrients that are not always available on the forest floor. While there are epiphytes in more temperate climates (most notably mosses and lichens), the nearly constant presence of water in the rainforest canopy provides an ideal environment for many epiphytic plants. Many plant families contain epiphytic species, but they are particularly abundant in the orchid (*Orchidaceae*) and bromeliad (*Bromeliaceae*) families.

It is estimated that well over 30,000 species of orchids exist on earth and that nearly 70% of those species are epiphytic. The orchid family has long been the subject of botanical intrigue, perhaps because of the flowers' exotic beauty and complex morphology. The oldest orchid in the Gardens' collection is an Asian *Coelogyne speciosa*, which has been at the institution since 1967. The addition of orchids collected by Gardens board members William and Mickie Thurston turned a few random plants into an important botanical collection. Over the span of many years, the Thurstons, along with noted orchidists friends, made repeated trips to Central and South America looking for new and unusual plants. Each collection was well documented, herbarium specimens were made, and duplicate divisions were distributed to a number of scientific and botanical institutions, including the Gardens. These early additions established an initial focus on several new world genera including *Encyclia* and *Oncidium*, but over the years the collection has diversified to include representative specimens from around the world, as well as man-made hybrids. Because of enthusiastic volunteers and a strong and active local orchid society, the collection has grown to well over 3,000 accessions representing more than 1,000 species from over 200 genera.

*Epidendrum parkinsonianum*

This bromeliad exhibits the characteristic whorled leaf arrangement typical of many plants from the family *Bromeliaceae*.

GARDENING WITH ALTITUDE: *Cultivating a New Western Style*

Bromeliads are members of a large family of plants native to tropical and semi-tropical areas of the western hemisphere. Often grown as houseplants, they are admired for their colorful, long-lasting flowers as well as their vase-shaped foliage. Many bromeliads grow in the shape of a rosette with overlapping leaves that form a central "cup" capable of holding large amounts of water. This water not only nourishes the plant in times of drought but also serves as a miniature ecosystem for various frogs, snakes and insects. Among the more recognizable bromeliads are the pineapple (*Ananas comosus*) and Spanish moss (*Tillandsia usneoides*). The Gardens' bromeliad collection was established in the 1970s by a major donation from Mrs. Walter R. Smith of New Orleans; many of the original plants are still in our collection. Look for the numerous bromeliads on display throughout both the Boettcher Tropical Conservatory and Cloud Forest Tree exhibits.

Many species of ferns have adopted an epiphytic way of life and have developed various strategies that enable them to survive high in the forest canopy. "Nest" ferns, such as *Asplenium* spp., form rosettes of leaves to catch leaf litter and humus, holding nutrients and water to nourish the plant. "Shield" ferns, such as the staghorn fern (*Platycerium bifurcatum*), have clasping basal leaves that provide a protected cavity where humus can accumulate. Other ferns simply have creeping rhizomatous roots that seek out accommodating nooks and crannies along the tree's surface.

Another remarkable group of epiphytes are the epiphytic cacti native to South and Central American rainforests. Unlike most cacti, which grow in arid desert conditions, epiphytic cacti in rainforests may receive up to 150 inches of rainfall each year. Some of the more familiar epiphytic cacti include the orchid cactus (*Epiphyllum* spp.), the Christmas cactus (*Schlumbergera* spp.) and the Easter cactus (*Rhipsalidopsis* spp.). A number of examples can be found in our displays, especially in Marnie's Pavilion.

*Vanda* Tokyo Blue 'Sapphire'

## Palms: Many Shapes and Sizes

When most people conjure an image of a palm tree, they picture a lone tree on a sandy beach silhouetted against tropical blue skies. In reality, palms come in many shapes and sizes and from a variety of habitats. Many have colorful "trunks," and others come armed with an amazing arsenal of spines.

Many gardens in tropical regions around the world boast incredible palm collections, but Denver's climate and the space limitations of our facilities do not allow us to have an extensive collection. Nevertheless, we have many rare and interesting specimens. In fact, there are more than 73 species from around the world on display. Among the more unusual palms we display are several specimens of ember palm (*Areca vestiaria*) from Sulawesi, Indonesia, which boast multiple stems with glowing orange color. The ruffle palm (*Aiphanes aculeata*) from South America and the salak palm (*Salacca magnifica*) from Borneo are covered with imposing spines to keep destructive jungle animals from destroying their canopies. Several species from the genus *Licuala* have thrived in our display, most notably the Australian fan palm (*Licuala ramsayi*) from Australia. *Bismarckia nobilis* grows natively in Madagascar, but its beautiful powder blue fronds have made it a popular landscape palm in warmer locales. One of the most striking palms in our collection is the white elephant palm (*Kerriodoxa elegans*) from southern Thailand. As the name implies, this palm has huge fronds with creamy white undersides, which are offset beautifully by the almost-black petioles (stems).

Since palms cannot be pruned, the limited height of the Boettcher Tropical Conservatory requires that some plants be removed before they reach full maturity. Others remain relatively small and could remain on display indefinitely. The Joey palm (*Johannesteijsmannia altifrons*) is a slow-growing palm that resides in the understory of tropical rainforests in Southeast Asia. Likewise, the dwarf fishtail palm (*Gronophyllum pinangoides*) from New Guinea and the lizard tail palm (*Iguanura spectabilis*) from Malaysia will maintain a short and compact growth habit. Although our palm collection may not be the biggest in the world, its diversity makes it well worth closer attention and study.

The trunk of the ruffle palm (*Aiphanes aculeata*) is covered with protective spines.

Joey palm (*Johannesteijsmannia altifrons*)

This anthurium (*Anthurium* sp.) flower clearly shows the petal-like spathe and projecting spadix found in all aroid flowers.

## AROIDS: OLD FRIENDS

Aroids, or *Araceae*, by any other name would be plants that nearly everyone would recognize. Many of the most commonly grown houseplants are from this family and cultivars can be found in homes, offices and shopping malls around the world. There are over 100 genera in this diverse plant family but *Philodendron*, dumb cane (*Dieffenbachia*) and Chinese evergreen (*Aglaonema*) are names that anyone who has grown a houseplant will likely recognize. Even plants with less recognizable names like elephant's ear (*Alocasia*), malanga or taro (*Xanthosoma*) and shingle plant (*Rhaphidophora*) still have the common characteristic that groups all these plants into one family. With *Araceae*, it is the spathe and spadix inflorescence. This plant family's two-part floral structure consists of the petal-like spathe and a projecting spadix that bears the actual flowers. While common to all aroids, this flower structure is more obvious in some than in others. It is common for windowsill-grown *Dieffenbachia* and *Philodendron* to bloom regularly, but because the flowers are relatively small and hidden by dense foliage, only the most observant will ever actually see them. On the other hand, who can miss the prominent flowers of *Anthurium* or *Spathiphyllum*?

Indeed, one of the largest flowers in the world is *Amorphophallus titanum*, also known as corpse flower. Native to Sumatra, corpse flowers can exceed ten feet in height and, as the common name suggests, the flowers emit a powerful smell of decaying flesh, which attracts carrion beetles for pollination. The Gardens' aroid collections include over 150 species from 31 genera, most of which are on display in the Boettcher Tropical Conservatory.

## Tropical Trees and Shrubs: A Burst of Bloom

On the surface, many tropical trees and shrubs may look remarkably similar, but periodically throughout the year a burst of flowers will appear that sets each plant uniquely apart. It is not uncommon for a plant to go completely unnoticed by visitors and staff until one day it suddenly bursts into bloom. Such is the case with many of the shrubs and trees in the Boettcher Tropical Conservatory.

There are many plant families that contain spectacular flowering trees and shrubs, but a few really stand out in our displayed collection. The acanthus family (*Acanthaceae*) is particularly showy and contains a number of plants that bloom sporadically throughout the year. Brazilian red cloak (*Megaskepasma erythrochlamys*) from Venezuela and Brazil can be covered with towering spikes of tubular white flowers surrounded by glowing red bracts (a modified leaf, like the red bracts on a poinsettia "flower"). Cardinal's guard (*Pachystachys coccinea*) and lollipop plant (*Pachystachys lutea*), both from northern South America, are close relatives from the acanthus family that also bloom throughout the year. The firecracker flower (*Crossandra infundibuliformis*) from southern India and Sri Lanka gets its common name from the cracking sound that can be heard when pods explode and shoot their seeds several feet from the parent plant.

The mallow family (*Malvaceae*) is well represented not only by a number of cultivated *Hibiscus* varieties but also by a wonderful specimen of Puerto Rico hibiscus (*Montezuma speciosissima*). The flowers of this wonderful small tree resemble soft-pink pendant hibiscus blooms. There is almost always a bloom or two to see, but occasionally the whole tree will burst into bloom at once.

The dogbane family (*Apocynaceae*) contains several incredibly fragrant flowering trees. Adam's apple (*Tabernaemontana crassa*) and stemmadenia (*Stemmadenia litoralis*) both bear their flowers high in the air and mostly out of view. Thankfully, their fragrance still reaches ground level where visitors can inhale a heavenly gardenia-like scent. Many of our more unusual flowering trees and shrubs are immature specimens and need a few more years to reach blooming size. Keep an eye to the sky on your next visit to the Boettcher Tropical Conservatory and see what's in bloom next.

Over the years, the Boettcher Tropical Conservatory and its associated collections have proved invaluable in executing the Gardens' mission of connecting people with plants. The Conservatory recreates a natural ecosystem that affords visitors new plants to see as well as an endless wealth of opportunities to learn. How lucky we are to have a tropical oasis in Denver.

Lollipop plant (*Pachystachys lutea*)

## A Cloud Forest in Colorado

In order to house orchids and bromeliads, a favorite part of the Gardens' early tropical plant collections, Marnie's Pavilion was constructed in 1981. Named in memory of Margaret E. "Marnie" Honnen, Marnie's Pavilion allows visitors the opportunity to view beautiful tropical specimens that had been hidden behind the scenes for so many years. As of 2003, Marnie's Pavilion is home to the Gardens' Cloud Forest Tree exhibit.

Epiphytes abound in a cloud forest ecosystem, and we have taken advantage of this new display environment to showcase many plants from our epiphyte collections. In addition to a continually changing display of orchids, many epiphytic bromeliads, ferns and tropical cacti are also on display.

Not all plants in a cloud forest are epiphytes. Although many people associate rhododendrons with temperate woodland gardens, there are many species native to tropical upland regions as well. Vireya rhododendrons (*Rhododendron laetum* and *Rhododendron zoelleri*) are two examples that can be found growing in the planting beds of the Cloud Forest Tree exhibit. Tropical carnivorous pitcher plants of the genus *Nepenthes* are another group of plants to be on the lookout for. *Nepenthes* naturally occur throughout tropical regions of Southeast Asia, and many of the most unusual and striking occur at higher altitudes. These amazing plants have modified leaf tips that form pitchers. Enzymes secreted by the plant into these pitchers attract insects that become trapped and are then digested. Look for all these and the many other small wonders in every nook and cranny of the Cloud Forest Tree exhibit.

Late afternoon sun streams through the mist in the Cloud Forest Tree exhibit.

> Marnie's Pavilion allows visitors the opportunity to view beautiful tropical specimens that had been hidden behind the scenes for so many years.

# A Daunting Job: Maintaining Tropical Collections and Displays

Maintaining such a large diversity of plants in one environment is a daunting job. While the basics of growing many of these plants is the same as if they were on a windowsill or in a sunroom at home, tending these same plants in a public garden frequented by hundreds of thousands of visitors each year presents unique challenges that must be dealt with on a day-to-day basis.

The foundation of any healthy plant is a strong and vigorous root system. To optimize root growth, the proper substrate must be provided. After renovations of the Boettcher Tropical Conservatory were completed in 1998, the native soil had been so compacted by construction equipment that the staff actually used jackhammers to break through the soil surface. A soil mix with plenty of organic material was added and incorporated into the top layer of heavy native clay soil. Each year, we add another layer of compost to the planting beds in a continuing effort to improve the soil and encourage strong and healthy root growth.

Every day of the year, the 12,000-square-foot Boettcher Tropical Conservatory is watered by hand. Not every plant uses the same amount of water, and hand-watering allows staff to adjust the amount of water applied to each individual plant as necessary. Water is applied at soil level and through the plant canopy to increase humidity, clean dust and debris from leaves, and to discourage pests.

In Colorado's dry climate, humidity becomes a critical factor in growing plants from a tropical rainforest environment. Humidity in the Boettcher Tropical Conservatory is increased with the use of an automated fog system, maintaining a humidity level of around seventy percent. Water purified by reverse osmosis is used to keep mineral deposits from clogging the tiny mist nozzles of the humidification system.

Temperatures in the Boettcher Tropical Conservatory are maintained between 65 and 85 degrees F, although Colorado's extreme weather conditions may push temperatures outside these parameters. During cold weather, perimeter fin-tube steam lines fueled by natural gas boilers provide heat. Cooling is achieved with humidification and by an evaporative system hidden behind the walls at the base of the facility.

Pitcher plant (*Nepenthes alata*)

Tropical soils are typically rather shallow in depth and do not hold a lot of nutrients. Fertilization is kept to a minimum, not only to replicate natural conditions but also to keep plants from growing too aggressively and outgrowing their limited space prematurely.

Because space is limited both horizontally and vertically, timely pruning is essential to keep all plants happy, healthy and in bounds. Each plant is inspected regularly, and appropriate trimming and pruning is employed as necessary. Proper pruning not only keeps plant growth in check, it also removes habitat for destructive insects and diseases as well as allowing plenty of light and air to penetrate to the lower plant layers.

In their tropic homelands near the equator, our plants would experience little change in day length throughout the year. In their northern home, day length and light become critical factors, especially during the shorter days of winter. It is during these months that special care must be taken to ensure enough light is reaching all the plants and that watering is adjusted accordingly.

Because there are few natural predators present in an enclosed system such as ours, insect pest populations can explode overnight. The Gardens strives to use as few chemicals as necessary to control pests and diseases. Instead, we utilize a variety of Integrated Pest Management (IPM) strategies. Rather than attempting complete eradication using potent chemical sprays, IPM involves using multiple techniques to keep pest infestations at lower, yet acceptable levels. Pruning and removal of infested material, removing pests by hand, or introduction of beneficial insects are just a few examples of control methods that do not expose visitors to toxic chemicals. While not introduced intentionally, there are a number of tree frogs and native Colorado toads that have taken up residence in the Boettcher Tropical Conservatory. They are each doing their part to control insect populations…and by the looks of their full bellies, they are finding more than enough to eat.

Maintaining the Boettcher Tropical Conservatory and behind-the-scenes collections is a labor of love for the staff and volunteers responsible for their care. While the workload is daunting, the rewards are vast. The Boettcher Memorial Tropical Conservatory, Marnie's Pavilion and their related collections are valuable tools in achieving the Gardens' mission, and the horticulture staff is proud to be connecting people with plants.

*Much of the work involved in maintaining the Gardens' tropical plant collections occurs behind the scenes in production greenhouses.*

## Decades of Planning and Building

Tropical plants have played an integral part in the Gardens' history and continue to be among the favorite attractions to thousands of visitors each year. Before the first formal garden was even completed at the Gardens, plans were underway for the construction of a state-of-the-art conservatory to showcase tropical plant collections in semi-arid Denver. In 1962, the Boettcher Foundation donated $10,000 to develop plans for a tropical conservatory and in 1963, donated an additional $1 million toward its construction. Architects Victor Hornbein and Edward D. White, Jr. and general contractor Gerald H. Phipps developed new and inovative ways to construct what has since become a Denver landmark.

During the two-year project, custom wood frames were constructed to allow concrete to be poured in place rather than in individual sections that would need to be seamed together later, and each row of Plexiglas™ panels was individually designed to fit the ever-changing trapezoidal windows, thus allowing condensation to run down the structural skeleton rather than dripping on the heads of visitors below. As construction progressed, mechanical systems to maintain optimum growing conditions were added, and rock and water features were installed. Finally, plants were added under the guidance of Conservatory Superintendent Ernest A. Bibee, and in January 1966 the Boettcher Memorial Tropical Conservatory was dedicated and opened to the public, greatly expanding the diversity of plants on display at the Gardens.

By the early 1990s, many vital systems in the Boettcher Tropical Conservatory were showing signs of decline and had become unreliable. Valuable plant collections were at risk, so planning began for a major renovation. Along with the architecture firm BIOS, Inc., staff and volunteers began brainstorming new botanical and educational themes, and drawings for the renovation were completed in 1997. Work began in January 1998 with the propagation and removal of existing plants, followed by demolition projects.

One of the major construction projects during this time was the creation of an artificial banyan tree, which encloses an elevator in order to improve access to all areas of the Boettcher Tropical Conservatory for visitors with physical limitations. Decks surrounding the tree provide viewing areas to the many diverse layers of the tropical rainforest exhibit. Additionally, new plants were acquired from around the country by Director of Horticulture James Henrich and Greenhouse Supervisor Gary Davis. When the Boettcher Tropical Conservatory reopened in the fall of 1998, more than 800 species of herbs, shrubs, trees and vines began to thrive in the lush tropical environment created by improved heating, cooling and humidification systems.

Parrot beak flower (*Heliconia orthotricha* 'Flash')

*The Cloud Forest Tree exhibit opened in January 2003 with a focus on displaying orchids, bromeliads and other epiphytic plants…*

With plants flourishing in the newly renovated Conservatory, it became apparent that improvements were needed in Marnie's Pavilion as well. In 2001, planning began to replace the formal plant displays in this space with a more naturalistic setting for the Gardens' epiphytic plant collections. The Cloud Forest Tree exhibit opened in January 2003 with a focus on displaying orchids, bromeliads and other epiphytic plants in a manner more closely resembling what one might find in nature. The "tree" is constructed of metal culvert pieces, rebar and Styrofoam covered with natural cork bark. Many of the plants growing on the tree are permanently attached, while others are rotated into the display as they come into bloom.

Over the years, the Boettcher Tropical Conservatory and its associated collections have proved invaluable in executing the Gardens' mission of connecting people with plants. In addition to the limitless educational opportunities, it also connects with people on a more emotional level. Children revel in the jungle atmosphere, and shrieks of laughter abound when school groups tour the exhibits. Visitors who have lived in warmer climates and now call Denver home often reminisce about the plants they once saw on a daily basis and now see here in their new homes. Often, visitors from tropical regions seem honored that we value plants from their homelands enough to grow and display them here in Denver. The Boettcher Tropical Conservatory's constantly evolving displays truly offer something for everyone.

*Visitors of all ages enjoy the diversity of plant life in the Boettcher Tropical Conservatory.*

A wide variety of epiphytes thrive on every limb of the Cloud Forest Tree.

Fragrant blooms from this *Plumeria* and from *Dendrobium* orchids (next page) are often used to make floral leis.

## Beyond Our Walls: A Conservation Challenge

Every day, thousands of acres of tropical rainforests are destroyed due to logging, ranching and mining. When the forest is cleared, more than trees are lost. Rainforests are home to more than half of the earth's total plant and animal species. When the plants are gone, the animals go with them. But the damage doesn't stop there. With no source for organic replenishment, the tropical soils quickly lose any soil nutrients they hold and become useless for agricultural crops. Tropical forests affect local and regional weather patterns and without the forests to mitigate massive rainfall, flooding reaches disastrous levels and water quality decreases downstream. Indeed, the loss of tropical forests affects the entire planet, contributing to increased global warming.

While rainforests are disappearing at an alarming rate, work is being done to slow the loss. Many countries now recognize the importance of these ecosystems and are establishing large national parks and preserves. Some local farmers are being paid premium prices for crops that are grown in a more sustainable manner.

The problem of tropical ecosystem degradation may seem overwhelming, but there are things that we all can do to help. Recycling aluminum cans helps reduce the amount of mining taking place in tropical forests. Make sure that any tropical products you consume (coffee, wood, ) were grown in a sustainable fashion, ensuring the environment can support production of these crops long into the future. Most importantly, educate yourself and others about the many contributions plants make in all our lives and the importance of ensuring these ecosystems are preserved.

## WAYS TO PROTECT THE ECOSYSTEM

- Recycle!
  *By recycling aluminum cans, you can help reduce the amount of mining taking place in tropical forests.*

- Read the label!
  *Make sure it indicates that any tropical products you consume (coffee, wood, chocolate) were grown in a sustainable fashion.*

- Educate yourself and others!
  *Learn about the many contributions plants make in all human lives and talk to your friends about the importance of ensuring these ecosystems are preserved.*

# VERSAILLES ON THE PLATTE

By Margaret Foderaro and Panayoti Kelaidis

*Centennial Gardens*

...Centennial Gardens is a delightful success that provides interest throughout the year.

The famed Versailles Gardens outside of Paris is the epitome of formal gardens. Designed by André Le Nôtre, landscape architect extraordinaire, at the request of King Louis XIV in 1662, the magical landscape of more than 225 acres has thousands of manicured trees and shrubs, great water basins with monumental statues, an orangerie, a vast collection of outdoor sculpture and some of the grandest fountains in the world.

It seems almost nonsensical to envision a Colorado version of Versailles. The two locations are literally worlds apart in all the critical components: the landscape, the climate, the soil, the available water and the native plant species. But former Denver Mayor Wellington Webb had just such a vision. Why shouldn't residents and visitors to Denver enjoy a similarly glorious formal garden on the South Platte River rather than the scene they were accustomed to viewing: a subsoil littered with unappetizing debris, crisscrossed by derelict railroad yards, and overrun by knee-high weeds.

The vision became a reality in the spring of 2003. The former dump is now a five-acre formal garden with neoclassical fountains, a sunken garden with water features, grand urns atop pedestals, hedges, native and nonnative dry-land plants, and a rainbow of flowering plants. Despite the improbability, the obstacles, the incongruence between the Platte River site and that of Versailles, and the severe drought of late 2001 and all of 2002, Centennial Gardens is a delightful success that provides interest throughout the year.

As the shrubs get ever thicker and blend into one another, and eventually even gain a sort of gnarly grace, and as the ground covers fulfill their purpose and blend seamlessly from bed to bed, we suspect that Centennial will become a favorite destination for Denverites and tourists. The next time you speed over Speer Avenue viaduct, take a detour west at the viaduct's apex and enjoy the largest formal garden we are aware of in the Rocky Mountain region. You will be beguiled by the lovely setting and find many plant and design ideas to take back to your home garden.

*The sound of water provides a whole new dimension in a formal garden.*

The wild beauty of roses (*Rosa* 'Linda Campbell') is the perfect foil for the trim lines and hedges.

## CENTENNIAL GARDENS: A CONCEPT AND A PLACE TRANSFORMED

The concept of the formal garden has been around for hundreds of years—although there are many variations on the basic idea. Formal gardens prominently feature art as much as plants and water. The artistic aspect of a formal garden includes design, hardscape (masonry work, woodwork and other non-plant elements in a landscape) and containers. The garden design features pathways, which create the parterre—an ornamental arrangement of flowerbeds or plots with intervening spaces of gravel or turf for walking. The pathways guide visitors to the beds and direct attention to them. Finally, of course, plants play an integral role in the design of a formal garden.

Much work was necessary to realize the vision of Centennial Gardens in arid Colorado. To begin, enormous amounts of soil had to be brought to the site to replace the badly polluted ground at what had been a dumping area for many years.

The drought that set in about the time the garden was envisioned cast a dark cloud over the plans. If it hadn't been for the scheme of translating the lush French garden into a water-smart western idiom of plants, the garden might have been shelved indefinitely during the extreme droughts of 2001-2002. Centennial Gardens was designed to use as little water as possible. The garden has both native and non-native dryland plants beautifully incorporated into the landscape but with a formal garden flair.

Spring crocus
(*Crocus vernus*)

## VISIT CENTENNIAL GARDENS AND LEARN THE FOLLOWING:

- Low-water gardening does not have to be naturalistic in style. You can use low-water plants in a formal setting with great success.

- Buffalo and other native grasses can be very effective. Many people have used them in home gardens as a replacement for turf. You can see how well it works in the highly stylized design of Centennial Gardens and try it in a garden of your own design—formal or informal.

- The Gardens are an outstanding primer for pruning and shaping techniques. Don't be afraid to try topiary at home.

- Study color and style in the four very carefully color-coordinated parterres. Notice how a stately garden style enables color to dazzle.

- Enjoy the rare pleasure of a formal garden experience that is extraordinary because of its environmental integrity.

Pansies (*Viola* x *wittrockiana* cvs.) provide winter color during warm spells from October through April.

Civitas, a leading local landscape architecture firm, designed elegant, rather neoclassical fountains and hardscape to frame the extensive planting beds. The floral design was conceived and executed by a team of Gardens' horticulture staff. Two broad terraced linden groves (*Tilia cordata* Greenspire® 'PNI 6025') are separated by a sunken garden with water features, containers, hedges and flowering plants. The grand urn-shaped containers atop pedestals placed in front of clipped green curly-leaf mountain mahogany hedges (*Cercocarpus ledifolius*) provide the garden with bold white accents. Visually, the fountains provide stability and balance, while the hedges unify the parterre garden with linden groves beyond.

Centennial Gardens is a treasure because of the daring combination of formality and the use of low-water demanding plants. The garden is ideally suited to Denver because of the attractive and versatile qualities of dry-loving, sun-loving and cold-hardy plant selections. Xeric dryland plants, the obvious choice, offer beautiful color, texture and structure all year round.

The decorative elements of formal gardens can range from benches to ornate containers to sculpted features on structures. At Centennial Gardens, the entry pavilion stands out as the foundation of the garden. It's a bold, broad expanse of Colorado sandstone, which calls the visitor to come closer and experience the garden from under its tall canopy. Benches beneath the pavilion offer visitors relief on hot summer days. The containers and their year-round seasonal displays add form and color to the garden. Two elegant 4-foot-tall urns welcome visitors at the front entrance to the garden, providing direction for guests.

Beneath the linden groves are shallow containers, which are, coincidentally, at eye level for a visitor who walks in the sunken sector of the garden. These containers are ablaze with the color of annuals during the summer and with dwarf upright spruces (*Picea glauca*) and pansies in the winter. Under the trimmed hedges, three different colors of rock mulch give a distinct dryland flavor to the garden. The rock mulches increase the visibility of the plants and assist in defining the patterns of the garden.

*The hedges of curly-leaf mountain mahogany (Cercocarpus ledifolius) take on maturity and grace.*

VERSAILLES ON THE PLATTE          CENTENNIAL GARDENS: A CONCEPT AND A PLACE TRANSFORMED

*Delphinium* Summer Skies Group are as beautiful up close as they are making blue and white towers of color in the garden.

Many who are familiar with formal gardens do not consider that nature has a role in the overall effect. But it does. A formal garden incorporates the surrounding environment into its finished design. At Centennial Gardens, many native riparian plants inhabit the edge of the nearby South Platte River, melding ironically with the drought-tolerant native plants within the garden. The linden groves also represent the naturalistic (or "wild") portion of the garden. In time, the lindens (*Tilia cordata* Greenspire® PNI 6025') will become a forest above the clipped curly-leaf mountain mahogany hedges (*Cercocarpus ledifolius*) and manicured buffalo grass (*Buchloe dactyloides* Legacy® and *B. dactyloides* 609).

The elaborate patterns of the flowerbeds offer a dramatic contrast to the wild side of the formal gardens. The plant material within these symmetrical and geometrical parterres is hedged, dead-headed and very tidy. Planting designs are organized into color schemes, creating, in effect, a tapestry spread on the ground. The colors of the rainbow are well represented from the red of *Rosa* 'Linda Campbell', the orange of daylily (*Hemerocallis* 'Chicago Sunrise') and the yellow of golden elderberry (*Sambucus nigra* ssp. *canadensis* 'Aurea'), to the blue of *Delphinium* Summer Skies Group and the purple of Rocky Mountain penstemon (*Penstemon strictus*). The green of green lavender cotton (*Santolina rosmarinifolia*) and the gray- and silver-colored foliage plants, such as lavender cotton (*Santolina chamaecyparissus*) and dwarf lavender (*Lavandula angustifolia* 'Hidcote' and *L. angustifolia* 'Munstead'), add balance to the brilliant shades.

Water, the final and essential element of a formal garden, plays a significant role: it soothes and consoles our spirits. The water features at Centennial Gardens are sculpture-like in appearance and classic in design, providing focal points to which our attention is drawn. They are situated in the pathways, enticing us to approach. Tranquility is felt throughout the garden but especially near the water. The glass-like surfaces of still pools reflect an eternity of blue sky while the gentle trickle of cascading water embodies the essence of time.

> Tranquility is felt throughout the garden…

> There is something of interest at all times of the year, especially in the winter…

## A GARDEN OF SEASONAL PLEASURES

Throughout the year, the garden offers visitors great and varied pleasures. The interplay between rigid borders of trimmed shrubs and bright colors contained within is, of course, much of the magic of formal carpet bedding and parterres. A succession of brightly colored flowers fill the beds from masses of pansies in the winter and spring months to more and more unusual bulbs in the summer and then the combinations of perennials, roses and annuals through the hot summer months. There is something of interest at all times of the year, especially in the winter when the cold gleaming architecture provides a foil to the softly textured winter foliage of all the various evergreen mounds, mats and trees.

The tension between the architectural framework and the flowery contents provides much of the delight at Centennial. Rob Proctor, the principal designer, has a tremendous sensitivity to color and combinations. Each of the four principal parterres at Centennial has a different color theme. The southeast panel consists of crimson flowers and deep purple foliage, and the northwest panel is lively dark red and yellow. The northwest corner has deep violet and orange, and the southwest quadrant features chartreuse, bright yellow and pale blue. Each panel glows and changes through the gardening year as different bulbs and perennials come into bloom.

Not only does Centennial boast the largest mass plantings we know of when it comes to native Rocky Mountain shrubs and perennials, it has quickly become a showcase of unusual bulbs as well. The chartreuse panel in the northeast corner of Centennial has hundreds of Juno irises (*Iris bucharica*) planted in dense clumps. The giant foxtail lilies (*Eremurus* 'Jeanne-Claire', *E.* x *isabellinus* 'Pinokkio' and 'Cleopatra') blaze in late spring and there are masses of unusual tulips and crocuses planted throughout the garden. The xeriscape conditions in this garden (occasional water, full exposure to the elements) seem to suit the bulbs especially well: they have clumped up in a short period of time and make a great splash in late winter and spring.

The emerging foliage of variegated iris leaves (*Iris pallida* 'Variegata').

Ice plant (*Delosperma* spp.) is colorful even in the winter months.

## THE WINTER LANDSCAPE

Two types of upright junipers add stark color to the garden in the winter: Rocky Mountain juniper (*Juniperus scopulorum* 'Wichita Blue') has a blue tint, and Chinese juniper (*Juniperus chinensis* 'Blue Point') has the traditional evergreen color. Ornamental grasses like the golden switch grass (*Panicum virgatum* 'Heavy Metal') withstand the winter weather (in particular, the snow) remarkably well; they sway in the wind on blustery cold days, and they stand out on a sunny or overcast day. Groundcovers like hardy ice plant (*Delosperma nubigenum*) and Turkish veronica (*Veronica liwanensis*) light up the garden with burgundy color in the winter.

Additional plants at the garden provide winter interest: cranberry cotoneaster (*Cotoneaster apiculatus*) and two varieties of crabapple, *Malus ioensis* 'Prairiefire' and *M.* 'Donald Wyman'. Both the cotoneaster and crabapples produce red fruits that afford extra color to the dormant plants. And we should not forget pansies. In Denver's Zone 5 climate, pansies do exceptionally well in the winter. They add well-needed color to the dormant soil and they are considered xeric, thereby not requiring very much water. They also do well in containers. Pansies (*Viola* x *wittrockiana* cvs.) come in a multitude of solid and mixed colors and most even have a lovely fragrance.

Colorado gardeners have learned that they can have a beautiful garden all year round by using ornamental grasses, conifers and perennials with flashy seed heads. At Centennial Gardens the staff does not cut back the ornamental grasses; rather they are left standing to give color, texture and height to the garden in these dormant months. Specimens that produce rosettes are especially eye-catching in the winter months. Examples are pincushion flower (*Scabiosa* 'Butterfly Blue'), pineleaf penstemon (*Penstemon pinifolius* and *P. pinifolius* 'Mersea Yellow') and avens (*Geum* 'Borisii').

GARDENING WITH ALTITUDE: *Cultivating a New Western Style*

Switch grass (*Panicum virgatum* 'Heavy Metal') makes a delightful see-through screen.

Versailles On The Platte

The Winter Landscape

Tulips (*Tulipa* 'Madame Lefeber') blaze brilliantly in the late winter sun.

## THE PROMISE OF SPRING

In the late winter and early spring, bright and perky bulbs greet visitors. In the fall of 2003 and 2004, the staff and volunteers planted more than 18,000 bulbs of *Iris*, *Fritillaria*, *Eremurus*, *Crocus*, *Tulipa*, *Hyancinthus* and *Muscari* at Centennial Gardens; 2006 will see over 30,000 bulbs blooming with bright color. These bulbs, in bloom from late February to June, range in color from the reds of *Tulipa* 'Golden Apeldoorn' and *Tulipa linifolia* to the blues of *Muscari* spp. and *Crocus chrysanthus* 'Blue Pearl'. Late winter bulbs such as crocus add color to the soil and dormant grass while the tall, majestic foxtail lily (*Eremurus*) adds height to the garden in late spring. Bulbs give the visitor hope that spring is just around the corner and add to the excitement and anticipation of the coming growing season.

## THE LIVELY AND INTENSE SUMMER

From mid-May to the beginning of June the main entry bed to the garden is blindingly intense because of the colors of four types of hardy ice plants: *Delosperma* 'John Proffitt', *Delosperma* 'Kelaidis', *Delosperma floribundum* Starburst™ and *Delosperma nubigenum*. The yellow and fuchsia pink hues of the flowers may make you reach for your sunglasses on a bright sunny day. The ground cover *Delosperma nubigenum* gives the earth a Granny-Smith-apple-green tone.

In the summer months, the garden is alive with sounds from the water features, movement from the many pollinators that visit the numerous flowers, and plants so vivid that you need to shade your eyes to admire them. The parterres, shaped like gigantic kaleidoscopes, change color as the bright red shrub roses meld into scarlet Peruvian verbena (*Glandularia peruviana*) and then reform to masses of *Salvia greggii*. At night, uplighting near the linden trees, the junipers (*Juniperus scopulorum* 'Wichita Blue'), and the entry pavilion offer the passerby intriguing views of these stately forms.

## THE STATURE OF AUTUMN

Red-bark lindens act as sentinels overlooking the garden in the fall. Most years they turn a rich old gold by October, and in the parterres below the hedges and ground covers take on burnished tints. This is the time when staff is busily adding yet more bulbs for the next spring's show. The pansies begin their yeoman's duty, blooming from autumn all the way to spring.

> Bulbs give the visitor hope that spring is just around the corner…

Hedges are a critical component of the formal garden.

## PLANTS FOR MORE THAN ONE SEASON

Some plants provide interest in more than one season. An ornamental grass that does well at Centennial Gardens is *Pennisetum alopecuroides* 'Hameln'. A gorgeous perennial both in the summer and winter is button snakewort (*Liatris spicata* 'Floristan Violett'). This plant has vivid purple blooms in July and produces seeds that make it a very attractive plant in the winter.

## THE ESSENTIAL HEDGES

Hedges are a critical component of the formal garden. At Centennial Gardens, the counterpart to the boxwood hedges at Versailles Gardens are the curly-leaf mountain mahogany (*Cercocarpus ledifolius*) and fernbush (*Chamaebatiaria millefolium*). Both plants are native to southwestern United States and are members of the rose family (*Rosaceae*). Mountain mahogany, an evergreen shrub with stark gray limbs and stems, sports new growth that is red. As the name of the fernbush indicates, its leaves are finely divided so that they look like ferns; the plants have small rose-like white flowers that attract hundreds of bees in the summer sun and give off a fragrance that is liked by some people but not by others. Additional hedges found in the garden are lavender (*Lavandula angustifolia* 'Hidcote' and 'Munstead'), both green and silver lavender cotton (*Santolina rosmarinifolia* and *S. chamaecyparissus*) and two barberries (*Berberis thunbergii* 'Aurea' and *B. thunbergii* Crimson Pygmy 'Atropurpurea Nana'). These hedges provide the necessary backdrop for the colorful manicured parterres.

Masses of Rocky Mountain zinnia (*Zinnia grandiflora*) fill in beneath the Rocky Mountain juniper (*Juniperus scopulorum* 'Wichita Blue').

On closer view, this *Rosa* 'Golden Unicorn' rewards the visitor with wonderful fragrance.

## THE GIFT OF FRAGRANCE

The garden gives us more than visual delights. Of the more than 150 different types of trees, shrubs, bulbs and forbs that dot the landscape of this formal garden, most of them give the olfactory senses much pleasure. In the red parterre, autumn sage (*Salvia greggii* 'Furman's Red') has the fragrance of sage, and a rose… is a rose; the third parterre relaxes the soul with 'Hidcote' and 'Mustead' lavender; the fourth parterre has the scent of a rose, *Rosa* 'Golden Unicorn'. As mentioned previously, the fernbush has a distinct odor that can't quite be defined. The flowers of the linden trees (*Tilia cordata* Greenspire® 'PNI 6025') give off such a sweet smell in June that the trees are always surrounded by bees, anxiously waiting to get the nectar being offered and, unbeknown to them, pollinating the flowers as they move from one to the next. Twenty-seven crabapple trees, *Malus* 'Donald Wyman' and *M. ioensis* 'Prairiefire', greet visitors before they enter the garden. In April, the flowers give off such a delightfully light fragrance that they attract some of the early pollinators. The smell of the three different varieties of junipers (*Juniperus scopulorum* 'Wichita Blue', *J. chinensis* 'Blue Point' and *J. squamata* 'Blue Star') evokes memories of hiking in the Colorado foothills.

Dewdrop on pansy blossom (*Viola* x *wittrockiana* cv.)

> …more than 80 different types of trees, shrubs, bulbs and forbs that dot the landscape… give the olfactory senses much pleasure.

VERSAILLES ON THE PLATTE — THE GIFT OF FRAGRANCE

*…Centennial Gardens has plants that have their origins from other parts of the world…*

## PUTTING DOWN ROOTS

When Versailles Gardens was initially planned, Louis XIV insisted on having full-grown trees planted in the *bosque* areas, or forest of trees. Beech and oak trees were uprooted from Normandy, transported in carts, and brought to Versailles where they were planted in anything but ideal soils and conditions. Similarly, Centennial Gardens has plants that have their origins from other parts of the world, namely Africa, Europe, Asia, the Middle East and South America. Hardy ice plants (*Delosperma nubigenum* and *D. cooperi*) hail from South Africa. These plants have daisy-like flowers that bloom from the end of May (*D. nubigenum*) to October (*D. cooperi*). These succulents open their flowers on sunny days, which number more than 300 per year in Colorado. Yellow ornamental onion (*Allium flavum*) hails from central Europe to western Asia. In the summer, this bulb features delicate yellow flowers hanging down like little bells. Two crocus species that have international origins are *Crocus chrysanthus* and *C. vernus* from Turkey and Europe, respectively. Although considered an annual plant in Colorado, red Peruvian verbena (*Glandularia peruviana*) does not die in some areas of the garden. As the name indicates, this plant had its start in the South American countries of Argentina, southern Brazil, Paraguay and Uruguay. Russian sage (*Perovskia atriplicifolia*) is a marvelous xeric plant with numerous purple flowers that bloom in late summer. The birth countries of this plant are Afghanistan and Pakistan. The Mediterranean region is also represented in this garden by lavender cotton (*Santolina rosmarinifolia*). The presence of non-native plants adds variety and depth to the garden and allows visitors to see that our steppe climate in Colorado is similar to places halfway around the world and to learn that plants that can grow in those countries can often grow here.

A bee's eye view of a spring crocus (*Crocus vernus*) reminds one that a garden is enchanting at all levels.

*Cranberry cotoneaster (Cotoneaster apiculatus) forms bold Fleur-de-lys pattern against the soft buffalo grass (Buchloe dactyloides)*

## LIVING WITH LESS WATER

Because the Denver metropolitan area receives on average about 15 inches of moisture per year, many plants must live here with little water, endure intense heat during the summer months at our high altitude, and be able to survive the freeze and thaw cycle of the winter months.

Centennial offers a xeric garden where visitors can see that while conserving water, they can still have a beautiful and colorful garden all year round. Bulbs give a spectacular show of color in late winter to late spring without much water. Because they have nutrients stored in the swollen portion that we call a bulb, they can survive, even thrive and naturalize, with minimal water. Junipers are inherently drought tolerant. They have survived some of the driest conditions in our state, even south-facing hillsides. Their scale-like leaves enable the plant to conserve moisture, making them an ideal plant for a full sun garden. Cranberry cotoneaster (*Cotoneaster apiculatus*), a native to Europe, Asia and north Africa, is a prostrate deciduous shrub with glossy leaves that does remarkably well at Centennial Gardens where it is planted in well-draining soil and full sun. In the fall, an abundance of red fruits hang from the delicate branches. Rocky Mountain zinnia (*Zinnia grandiflora*), a native to southwestern United States, has yellow-orange flowers. This amazing plant blooms well into October, uses very little water, and attracts numerous pollinators like bees and butterflies. However, it does come out of dormancy later than other perennials, so give it a chance before you conclude that it is dead.

Warm-weather turf grasses, like buffalo grass (*Buchloe dactyloides* Legacy® and *B. dactyloides* 609), are best for our semi-arid region. These grasses turn green in late spring and go dormant in early fall, thus not requiring water for one month in the spring and fall. The leaf blade, a soft, sage green in the summer and red in the fall, is very narrow and delicate looking as it billows in the wind. By planting numerous crocus bulbs in the fall in your buffalo grass, you will add a bit of color to your grass in late winter. Over time, the crocuses will naturalize, becoming a rainbow of color in a sea of green.

> …many plants must live here with little water, endure intense heat during the summer months at our high altitude, and be able to survive the freeze and thaw cycle of the winter months.

# THE PUBLIC GARDEN AS SCIENCE
By Thomas Grant and Dr. Anna Sher

Entering the canyon is a commitment. There are steep rock walls that must be scaled, and it will take time to reach the remote location of the rare thistle we are seeking. Rock-climbing gear may not be necessary for our trip, but there is an old climbing rope dangling from a bolt in a nearby cliff band and a monument to a child who fell off the cliff years ago. The site of our risky climb is Cross Mountain Canyon in northwestern Colorado, one of few locations on earth where Ownbey's thistle (*Cirsium ownbeyi*) can be found. This rare, native thistle grows on the precipitous walls of the deep canyon that was carved through Cross Mountain by the Yampa River. When we first started visiting the site, we would swim in the mouth of the canyon after completing our work, always being careful not to get sucked into the currents that quickly became a class-four rapid. In the recent drought years we could walk into the canyon and wade through areas that previously had thrilled river rafters.

> The site of our risky climb is Cross Mountain Canyon in northwestern Colorado, one of few locations on earth where Ownbey's thistle (*Cirsium ownbeyi*) can be found.

Denver Botanic Gardens research staff descends into Cross Mountain Canyon, site of the rare Ownbey's thistle (*Cirsium ownbeyi*).

Photograph–Denver Botanic Gardens

## Why Make Perilous Journeys?

As plant ecologists, our main reason for trekking to the site was to study the interactions of an introduced insect (*Rhinocyllus conicus*) on the rare thistle (*Cirsium ownbeyi*). Although a swim in the river is a nice way to end a long day of squatting in order to identify and measure the rare thistle, don't let the incredible surroundings fool you. This is hard work and often we fail to achieve our goals of finding and conserving the rarest plants.

In this case, the introduced insect is a seed-boring weevil, a type of beetle that was purposefully introduced to the western United States to control another introduced species, musk thistle (*Carduus nutans*). The larvae of the weevil use the developing seeds of thistles as food, thereby reducing the production of viable seeds, which, presumably would cause the populations of the thistles, rare or invasive, to decrease. What an interesting concept! We introduce a species to a different continent to control a non-native thistle that was previously introduced and has become weedy or noxious or, some might say, obnoxious. The use of biocontrols is controversial, having both successes (such as the Australian control of invasive *Opuntia* cacti), and, naturally, failures. In the case of the native and non-native thistles of North America, we would consider this biocontrol project something of a failure, because it has not successfully controlled the invasive musk thistle and has had negative impacts on several native thistles.

A plant conservationist's bias is toward protecting the native and rare plants, thereby supporting the integrity of natural functioning ecosystems, while finding ways for humans to coexist with nature. Fortunately, the use of biocontrols has advanced from the initial introduction of this weevil in 1969 to a more advanced and systematic process of determining exactly what the insect will eat and evaluating the potential risks on natural vegetation and an ecosystem's web of interactions.

The use of introduced biocontrol insects is only a small portion of our current land management practices on earth's natural and developed environments. Historically, land management practices focused on the extraction of resources for use by our growing human population. Now, we are beginning to understand the complex relationships of the planet's environment and incorporate these practices in our management policies with the goals of supporting humanity, while sustaining nature. In the case of Ownbey's thistle, we hope we are not too late to make a positive difference with proactive science, management and conservation.

Evidence of insect damage to Ownbey's thistle (weevil larvae boring hole and eggs upon the involucral bracts).

Ownbey's thistle (*Cirsium ownbeyi*) in flower.

## THINGS TO CONSIDER

- Recognize the interrelationships of all life on earth. Everything is interconnected in the incredibly complex web of life.

- Educate yourself about the importance of protecting native and rare plants. Consider the myriad of species–including humans–that rely upon plants for food or shelter.

- Think of ways for humans to coexist with nature by understanding the consequences of different land management strategies. In the context of plant conservation, support land management practices that strive for balance between human needs and all the natural environments affected. Whose needs matter most: humans' or those of wildlife and flora? Sometimes it appears that these two "interest groups" are in conflict. However, it becomes increasingly clear that the fates of all living things on the planet are linked. The more pertinent question is whether we have the luxury of considering long-term sustainability for all living things while there are so many immediate pressing needs of humans that are more likely to be in conflict with "nature." The answer will depend on our values.

## A Story of One Invader

Dawn is quietly breaking on another clear summer's day; alas it is too quiet, considering the sounds one expects from a streamside forest. A hum of mosquitoes, the scurry of a rat over the salty detritus and the occasional call of a house finch are all that can be heard. What was once a majestic cottonwood-willow bosque with nesting bald eagles, flocks of cranes and roaming coyote has been transformed into a monoculture of weeds, most notably invasive tamarisk (*Tamarix* spp.), also commonly called saltcedar. It towers overhead with networks of ruddy, strong stems and dense, scaly foliage. These leaves are equipped with salt glands to handle the saline river water, and when the branches fall to the ground, these leaves create soil so "hot" as to prevent most other plants from germinating. Of course, plants couldn't germinate anyway; it is too dark under the shrub-like trees. Because it is summer, many trees are fringed with coral-pink and white foam of millions of tiny flowers.

As the day warms, bees begin their work on the copious flowers. Not much else is blooming this time of year in the West, when conditions are mostly dry. The river didn't flood much the previous spring, so it did not prepare any natural sites for the germination of seeds of the cottonwood and willow that still make it to these reaches; those seeds, embedded in tufts of "cotton" floating on a breeze or in the water, do not find a home. A few older trees are left, poking up above a canopy of tamarisk, but no young cottonwoods are around to take their places when the decadent trees eventually fall with age or collapse in the hot fires the tamarisk litter promotes.

It's not the tamarisk's fault, of course. Humans brought it in from Asia as an ornamental, and land managers planted it extensively in the mid-1900s. It has done very well to secure riverbanks and provide food for honeybees. When no other plants could survive the harsh soils, the lack of spring flooding or our appetite for wood, the sturdy tamarisk was able to take its place as the new western-river dominant, alongside a suite of other weedy plants such as cheatgrass (*Bromus tectorum*), perennial pepperweed (*Lepidium latifolium*), Canada thistle (*Cirsium arvense*) and leafy spurge (*Euphorbia esula*). Although some of these species were unintentional hitchhikers, it is estimated that 5,000 of our current "noxious weeds" were intentionally brought in, many by European gardeners wanting a bit of the Old Country in their new American homestead. Just as introduced insects directly threaten rare species, so too do literally thousands of non-native plant species. Biocontrol may be a viable option for tamarisk, but bringing new organisms to an ecosystem must be done with caution, as we see in the case of the thistle weevil.

Copious flowers of the invasive tamarisk tree (*Tamarix ramosissima*) made it a popular ornamental.

An example of the under-story of tamarisk, which is too salty, dry and dark for other plants to grow.

Dried tamarisk flower-buds of a herbarium specimen at Denver Botanic Gardens' Kathryn Kalmbach Herbarium.

THE PUBLIC GARDEN AS SCIENCE  A STORY OF ONE INVADER

A hydro-axe equipped bulldozer grinds down a thicket of tamarisk around a young cottonwood tree at a research site in Florence, CO.

Shrubby tamarisk trees with fall foliage invade and degrade a drainage in the Upper Colorado River Basin. Only a few decadent cottonwoods remain at this site.

The mulch that remains may assist in establishing native plants.

As botanic gardens fulfill the mission of expanding our understanding of plant diversity, exposing us to worldly delights we may otherwise not know existed, there is a new awareness of the risks of introducing plants. The vast majority of "exotic" species never pose a risk, and it can be argued that most of those that do become invasive are simply taking advantage of poor stewardship on our part (such as is likely in the case of the tamarisk). Overgrazing, over-logging, road-building, damming of rivers and other human activities necessary for economic development sometimes come at a steep price: loss of ecological integrity. Changing soil, water or standing vegetation in a system can have seemingly endless and cascading ramifications, including decreased water and air quality, reduction in land uses and value to humans, and loss of biodiversity. We may not even notice the harm to ecological balance until the weeds (the natural expression of this change) take over and cause their own problems.

Thus, researchers and staff at botanic gardens around the country are playing an ever-increasing role in righting the balance—not only by heading efforts to remove invasive weeds from natural areas but also by addressing some of the cause of harm (land management) and the impacts of various management choices (such as biocontrol). In this way, both the symptom and the disease can be treated.

Back at our tamarisk infestation, we fast-forward to the next spring. Changes are afoot. The sound of engines can be heard in the distance, and clouds of dust herald the approach of heavy machinery. Escorted by two pickup trucks and SUVs emblazoned with State Agriculture and Denver Botanic Gardens logos, a monster bulldozer appears, armed with grinding blades to remove tamarisk. The removal team unloads from the vehicles but gives the dozer wide berth as it begins its tough work of grinding the great trees to the ground. Chunks of wood go flying as the axe-head spins and cuts. The removal of tamarisk is done in strips perpendicular to the river, so that a research team can monitor the effects of different control efforts. Some strips will be sprayed with herbicide, and others left alone.

Both the operator of the dozer and the owner of the land grew up in these parts. During a break the two men swap fond memories of hunting and fishing in the area, which is no longer possible. They also confirm the suspicion of the research leader: the weed-encroached surrounding land was very heavily grazed when it was dominated by native grasses and wildflowers. Now the hills are mostly cacti and shrubs until the land meets the riparian strip of dense tamarisk. It is no longer good for cattle, much less native wildlife.

> Overgrazing, over-logging, road-building, damming of rivers and other human activities necessary for economic development sometimes come at a steep price: loss of ecological integrity.

Restoration research on 12 native species, which will be used in re-vegetation after tamarisk removal. Graduate students from the University of Denver, Robin Bay, and the University of Colorado at Denver, Carol Winther, assist in monitoring plant growth.

Back at the Gardens, a search on the herbarium's database reveals which species were found in the area before the tamarisk. These invaluable records give us a snapshot of changes to these ecosystems over time. The mycological herbarium tells us which mushrooms are native in the area as well.

"Weeding" this site of tamarisk will not be enough. Our previous scientific work has shown that re-vegetation of these natives will be necessary to keep out the tamarisk and bring back the eagles, butterflies and wildflowers once known here. Enter teams of volunteers, students and Gardens staff, armed to the nines with the tools of the trade: shovels, bags of seed and bright flagging to demarcate various re-seeding techniques. They split into groups responsible for different tasks: some will prepare the sites by hand-pulling new weeds, others will compile site information on clipboards, and still others will spread the mixture of native grass and forb seed. They know that the strips treated with herbicide will have fewer re-grown tamarisk but also will be much more difficult to re-vegetate. The seed mixture includes native legumes, which may be able to deal with the herbicide remaining in the soil. Students from a local university are using this project as the basis of their graduate theses; one has been researching the use of beneficial fungal spores for repairing the soil. This latter work was a greenhouse study funded by the Bureau of Reclamation and conducted at the Gardens. These partnerships between the Gardens, the public, government agencies and academic institutions make such large-scale projects possible and likely to succeed.

As the sun rises, so too does the temperature, but this morning shift is done. Drinking water from a cooler, we relax in the shade of one of the few remaining cottonwood trees. It will be at least a year before we know if this re-vegetation work is successful; it looks to be a wetter year than the previous one, which will be good for seed germination; but some of these species may not become well established in the plant community for a few plant-generations. At this site, we're trying several native grasses, including slender wheatgrass (*Elymus trachycaulus*), creeping wild rye (Leymus triticoides), western wheatgrass (Pascopyrum smithii) and alkali sacaton (Sporobolus airoides), plus the legume purple crownvetch (Coronilla varia).

It is hoped that these species can be used to balance the needs of range managers who want forage for cattle with the need to repair the ecosystem as a whole and restore it to some semblance of what it was. Once the flows have a chance to return somewhat to this drainage, there should be enough native seed of the remaining trees (as well as other species) for them to come back on their own. Research has shown that seedling native trees compete well against invading seedling tamarisk, which is yet more evidence that if we give the native system a chance, it can be resilient to some forms of invasion.

The tree under which we rest is a female cottonwood; the drooping strands of green flowers have just become apparent. Across the drainage is a male with much more obvious red tassles hanging at the tips of branches, swaying in the breeze that will carry the pollen to this and other waiting females. Since there is no need for bees, the female flowers are neither scented nor colorful; scent and color are energetically expensive adaptations to attract animal pollinators. In a month or so, the female flowers will ripen into round fruits. These will crack open, filling the air with the tufts of "cotton" embedded with seed; thus, the tree earns its name: cottonwood. Everywhere there is wet soil and light, the seed may germinate and establish another small sapling. The willows here also generate wind-dispersed seed and have similar germination requirements.

Cottonwood and willow trees are keystone species to this ecosystem, securing riverbanks and providing habitat for nesting birds and other animals, while allowing enough light to penetrate to support a diverse understory of herbaceous growth. Although tamarisk is used by some species (particularly cup-nesting birds such as the southwestern willow flycatcher), it is hardly the foundation of a thriving native ecosystem. And we humans, of course, prefer the open space and welcome shade to the close quarters under the tamarisk trees. We can begin to imagine this bosque transformed into the gallery forest it once was, with wildflowers in springtime and native wildlife aplenty. It's a big job, but playing doctor to ecosystems is what we're about. Making room for native plants is only the first step.

Successful restoration of a dense tamarisk infestation to a native cottonwood bosque.

## Connecting People and Plants: The Role of Botanic Gardens

Throughout the world, staff at botanic gardens are realizing the importance of plant conservation and restoration programs, possibly because the world seems to get smaller and smaller while the human population and our needs continue to grow. The relationship and dependence of humans on plants, both wild and agricultural, cannot be ignored or understated any longer. The importance of plants is obvious: They are the food we eat, they create the oxygen we breathe, our forests sequester atmospheric carbon and plants are an essential component of our natural ecosystems. Plants form the basis of most life, and modern human society is beginning to realize the critical and complex relationship between plants, humans and all life on earth. Unlike traditional cultures, where lives depended directly on plants and the local environment, modern society has become removed from the basic processes that sustain life. Plant conservation is all about connecting people and plants, while providing balance between our needs and those of the environment.

Botanic gardens are in a unique position to facilitate conservation work and partnerships between governments, academia and most importantly the environmentally aware citizens of the world. The humanitarian goals of the organizations involved in social and environmental issues are staggering, yet the scope of environmental sustainability needs to broaden dramatically. Envision a day when every decision made by the world's corporate and political bodies is based on an evaluation of the long-term effects on the environment and all humans. Imagine a day on which decisions that are made respect life of all kinds and promote practices that strive for balance, equality and environmental sustainability. Botanic gardens bridge the gap between the diverse human groups that dictate how our limited resources are utilized; those gardens weave the human and botanical relationship. As the human footprint on earth expands, our knowledge increases, our understanding grows and the realization of our responsibility to the environment becomes undeniable. The rationale for conservation could be human or eco-centric, as long as we acknowledge the relationship and reliance between humans and our environment.

Conservation programs at botanic gardens have the opportunity to integrate the public's love of plants with scientific information and with the partnerships to make a difference. There are a wide variety of plant conservation programs that botanic gardens can be involved in. Historically, botanical institutions worked primarily in plant exploration, systematics or taxonomy. These activities formed, respectively, the foundation for discovering the diversity of the world's flora, identifying the relationships between plants and developing names for every unique species. During much of the last 500 years, botanic gardens were the primary source of plant information

> The importance of plants is obvious: They are the food we eat, they create the oxygen we breathe, our forests sequester atmospheric carbon and plants are an essential component of our natural ecosystems.

and herbal medicines. However, the foci of most botanic gardens' research or plant conservation programs have changed dramatically since then. Today, gardens work closely with governments, universities and the public to study, conserve and restore the earth's remaining natural plants and ecosystems.

Central to the mission of any botanic garden seeking to understand and preserve biodiversity will be the maintenance of an excellent herbarium. At Denver Botanic Gardens, there are two collections of the region's native flora and fungi that are used to document and study the diversity of these life forms: the Kathryn Kalmbach Herbarium of Vascular Plants (1943) and the Denver Botanic Gardens Herbarium of Fungi (1965). Herbaria, plural for herbarium, are similar to libraries, but instead of books the collections are plants or fungal specimens with detailed information about what they are, and when and where they were collected. Herbaria form the primary historical records that the world has of a plant species' diversity and distribution. In addition to the critical historical information, herbaria are often used to assist botanists in the determination of a plant's identity or to acquire plant material that can be used for genetic analysis as plant geneticists rework our understanding of the relationships between plants. Keeping these collections current is tireless and patient work; to say that it requires individuals who are passionate about plants is an understatement. Both of the Gardens' herbaria were founded by such-minded volunteers, and these dedicated botanists and mycologists remain essential to their operation.

At the Gardens, our active plant conservation work began in the early 1990s, primarily in partnership with the Center for Plant Conservation (St. Louis, MO) to collect, grow and store seeds of the rarest plants in the southern Rocky Mountains. Originally, seed banking was the primary goal, but this wasn't enough. Scientific studies of the causes of a species' rarity and restoration efforts to prevent extinction were the obvious next step. Our projects quickly extended into the realm of rare plant population studies (demographics), invasive species control and ecosystem restoration.

Our excursion into the canyon for Ownbey's thistle is an example of rare plant projects in the natural habitat, or "in-situ". We study some of the most uncommon species of the central and southern Rocky Mountains to understand population fluctuations and determine potential threats. These demographic studies are similar to a human population census and the data is used to create statistical population models that can incorporate natural or anthropogenic events, such as drought or human destruction, respectively. The demographic studies can determine a plant population's growth rate (increasing or decreasing) and approximately how long it will be before that plant could become extinct, due to their limited number of individuals. This type of analysis falls under the category of population viability analysis or determination of a minimum viable population, since small populations are more susceptible to extinction.

Ex-situ conservation focuses on removing plants or seeds from the wild for inclusion in a seed bank or a living collection at a botanic garden. In conjunction with the Center for Plant Conservation, the Gardens has over 30 of the rarest species in the region in long-term storage at the National Center for Genetics Resources Preservation in Fort Collins, Colorado.

Plant specimens are carefully pressed, preserved and recorded at Denver Botanic Gardens' vascular plant and fungal herbaria.

Denver Botanic Gardens staff collects soil moisture measurements at the Rabbit Mountain Open Space in northern Boulder County.

Additional germination studies and propagation occur as the seeds are placed in long-term storage at −18 degrees C or in extremely cold liquid nitrogen (-196 degrees C). These aspects of an ex-situ conservation program provide the knowledge to propagate the species (which is essential for potential reintroduction to the wild) or to reduce the need to collect additional plant material from the wild for research. Without a genetic reserve of the rare species in a seed bank or living collection, we have no options if the species goes extinct in the wild. An often-overlooked benefit of an ex-situ conservation program is the ability to display and interpret these rare organisms to the public for educational purposes. Many of our region's rare plants have interesting stories that naturally involve humans and our use, or misuse, of the earth's natural resources.

Our work with tamarisk and plants to replace it is an example of ecological restoration. This field is a fairly new science, and is as much an art form. It can be very difficult to restore a degraded, weed-infested landscape to a resilient and functioning natural ecosystem. Ecological restoration can be viewed as an umbrella science under which the Gardens' rare and invasive species projects are essential players, since the protection of rare plants and the control of invasive weeds are often primary objectives of a restoration project. The Gardens' restoration projects involve the use of all available techniques, including fire (prescribed burns), herbicides, biocontrols, native seed collection and propagation, and lots of volunteers. The scope of restoration work needed could not be addressed without the incredible commitment of volunteers.

## It's Our Choice

Currently, it is believed that more than 250,000 species of plants exist on earth; this is likely to be a gross underestimate if the tropical regions of the planet are thoroughly explored before they are destroyed. It would be an understatement to say that humans have reduced the natural biodiversity of the world. Which is more diverse: a parking lot or a ponderosa pine forest? Which is more interesting, and most importantly, which is more valuable? The last question is an easy one to answer if you consider the value of the timber and the potential greenhouse gases it absorbs, or the role of the forest in providing clean air, food and habitat for the birds, rodents and humans that call it home. Of course, there is also the value we associate with the pleasure of hiking through the ponderosa forest or smelling its butterscotch-scented bark. Once you realize the inter-relationships of all life on earth, it can be difficult to ignore our effect on the other species that also call it home. The world is changing dynamically and more than six billion humans are driving many of these changes. The question is what will humans decide to value and what will we decide to protect.

Successful reintroduction of the rare prairie gentian (*Eustoma grandiflorum*) at the Rocky Mountain Arsenal National Wildlife Refuge.

# Appendix I: About the Authors

**Margaret Foderaro**
Margaret was a horticulturist at Denver Botanic Gardens for five years where she designed the Sacred Earth garden, which focuses on plants used by American Indians from the Colorado Plateau. She also helped with the design of The Birds and Bees Garden. For almost two years, Margaret managed Centennial Gardens, which features native and non-native plants in a formal French design. She also taught botany classes, hosted lectures and wrote articles for the Gardens. She is a member of the Colorado Native Plant Society and the Rocky Mountain Chapter of the North American Rock Garden Society.

**Mark Fusco, Senior Horticulturist**
Mark has worked at Denver Botanic Gardens since 1997 in a number of capacities. A degree in Landscape Design from Colorado State University led to the involvement in the development of three gardens at Denver Botanic Gardens, with his primary focus on western native plants and Colorado alpine plants. Mark designed and built the troughs in Wildflower Treasures and is responsible for the design and construction of the Alpine Rock Garden at Mount Goliath. In addition, Mark designed and project managed the implementation of June's PlantAsia. He teaches classes and gives lectures on the subjects of Asian plants and gardens, trough gardening and western native plants.

**Tom Grant, Manager of Research Programs**
Tom has managed research programs at Denver Botanic Gardens since 1997. His primary focus is on rare plant monitoring projects, ex-situ plant conservation and ecosystem restoration projects. At the Gardens, he is involved in educating the public about environmental issues, both through the development of volunteer ecological restoration opportunities and plant conservation based interpretation. He is a primary organizer in the Colorado Rare Plant Symposium, where experts discuss priority rare plant issues. Tom also serves on the advisory board for the Center for Native Ecosystems; is a peer-reviewer for the U.S. Forest Service's species assessment program; and was the primary organizer of Partners for Colorado Native Plants, a grassroots collaboration dedicated to researching and restoring Colorado's native plant communities. He teaches several botany-related classes, as well as training courses for volunteers on rare plant surveying, use of global positioning systems (GPS) and *Orchidaceae* morphology.

**Dan Johnson, Curator of Native Plants**
Dan has been gardening for as long as he can remember, and his years of experience and formal training now include eight years with Denver Botanic Gardens' Horticulture Department, currently as Curator of Native Plant Collections. When time allows, he travels throughout the West and Southwest in search of unusual and underused natives for trial in Colorado's rigorous climate. Occasional forays to similar regions of the world help to further broaden the palette of plants suitable for western gardens. He has created some of Denver Botanic Gardens' most beautiful and self-sustaining gardens, celebrating its sense of place with a focus on resource conservation and horticultural diversity. His passion for plants and love of the Western landscape are both expressed as he designs and maintains the majority of the Gardens' extensive native and xeric gardens.

**Panayoti Kelaidis, Director of Outreach**
Panayoti has worked at the Gardens for 25 years in many capacities. His far-reaching knowledge of horticulture in the mountainous and dry climate of Colorado has aided Panayoti in co-managing the Plant Select program, which is a plant introduction program where he has helped discover and name numerous plants, as well as disseminate nearly 6 million plants. Panayoti designed the plantings for the world-renowned Rock Alpine Garden and helped implement Wildflower Treasures, South African Plaza and the Romantic Gardens among many other gardens at Denver Botanic Gardens. He is a past president of the Rocky Mountain Chapter of the American Rock Garden Society as well as the American Penstemon Society, and serves on many professional horticulture society boards. Panayoti is the recipient of the Award of Excellence from National Garden Clubs and the Arthur Hoyt Scott Medal from Swarthmore College, which is generally considered the highest honor in American horticulture.

**Dr. Anna Sher, Director of Research, Herbaria and Records**
Dr. Sher splits her time between the Gardens and the University of Denver, where she is a Professor of Conservation Biology. She has published research in several journals, including *Conservation Biology* and *Ecological Applications*. She is an expert in invasive species, especially the tamarisk, and has been appointed by Colorado Governor Bill Owens to the advisory group mandated to control this species. Dr. Sher has conducted research in Israel as a Fulbright award recipient, investigating the community-level response of desert annual plants to competition across productivity gradients. She has also spent extensive time in Kenya, doing research and leading semester abroad programs to teach American college students about the East African ecosystem and conservation. Dr. Sher also directs the Applied Plant Conservation Training Program, a collaborative institute with the U.S. Botanic Gardens. Her current research focuses on the restoration of native ecosystems after tamarisk control.

**Nick Snakenberg, Curator of Orchids**
Nick has worked at Denver Botanic Gardens since 1993 in an array of capacities. A graduate of Iowa State University with a Bachelor of Science degree in Horticulture, he currently curates the Gardens' orchid collection and helps manage the Boettcher Memorial Tropical Conservatory and its associated tropical collections. He has taught many horticultural classes for the Gardens and is a frequent speaker for local garden clubs and plant societies. His affiliations with professional organizations add to his expertise and include membership in the Orchid Digest Corporation, Encyclia Enthusiasts, the Association of Educational and Research Greenhouse Curators, and the American Association of Botanical Gardens and Arboreta. He is a past president of the Denver Orchid Society and is a member of the American Orchid Society and serves on its Education Committee. Nick is currently a student judge with the Rocky Mountain Judging Center in the American Orchid Society's orchid judging program.

**Joe Tomocik, Water Gardens Curator**
Joe has been responsible for the internationally acclaimed Water Gardens collection at Denver Botanic Gardens since 1982. He spearheaded the Gardens' development into the water gardening Mecca of the United States. Joe founded the world's first water gardening society, the Colorado Water Gardening Society (CWGS), in 1983. Each year, this society provides the labor and expertise in creating and dismantling the Gardens' elaborate storied displays. Joe has cooperated with leading hybridizers and nurseries in naming and introducing a number of outstanding award-winning waterlilies, including *Nymphaea* 'Denver's Delight', *N.* 'Colorado' and *N.* 'Joey Tomocik'. He received the International Water Gardening Society's Hall of Fame Award in 1997, and he is past President of the Rocky Mountain Regional Turfgrass Association. His highly respected and ever-growing outreach program has helped to establish many outstanding water gardens, including the stunning garden at the University of Denver. Additionally, his articles have appeared in prestigious magazines including *Horticulture* and *Fine Gardening*.

# APPENDIX II: ADDITIONAL RESOURCES

## GOING NATIVE IN THE GARDENS

**Books**

Barr, Claude A.
*Jewels of the plains.*
(Minneapolis: University of Minnesota Press, 1983).

Kelly, George, W.
*Rocky Mountain horticulture is different: How to modify our climate to fit the plants, and how to select plants to fit our climate.*
(Denver: Green Thumb Council, 1951).

Springer Ogden, Lauren.
*The undaunted garden: Planting for weather-resilient beauty.*
(Golden, CO: Fulcrum Publishing, 1994).

Tannehill, Celia and Jim Klett.
*Best perennials for the Rocky Mountains and high plains.*
(Fort Collins, CO: Department of Horticulture and Landscape Architecture, Colorado State University, 2002).

Weber, William A. and Ronald C. Wittmann.
*Colorado flora: Eastern slope.*
(Boulder, CO: University of Colorado Press, 2001).

Weber, William A. and Ronald C. Wittmann.
*Colorado flora: Western slope.*
(Boulder, CO: University of Colorado Press, 2001).

Winger, David, ed.
*Xeriscape color guide: 100 water-wise plants for gardens and landscapes.*
(Denver and Golden, CO: Denver Water and Fulcrum Publishing, 1998).

**Web sites**

Plant Select:
www.ext.colostate.edu/psel/index.html

Planttalk:
www.ext.colostate.edu/ptlk/index.html

## TALE OF THE TUNDRA

**Books**

Duft, Joseph F. and Robert K. Moseley.
*Alpine wildflowers of the Rocky Mountains.*
(Missoula, MT: Mountain Press Publishing, 1989).

Gellhorn, Joyce.
*Song of the alpine: The Rocky Mountain tundra through the seasons.*
(Boulder, CO: Johnson Books, 2002).

Williams, Jean, ed.
*Rocky Mountain alpines: Choice rock garden plants of the Rocky Mountains in the wild and in the garden.*
(Portland, OR: Timber Press, 1986).

Wingate, Jan and Loraine Yeatts.
*Alpine flower finder: The key to Rocky Mountain wildflowers found above timberline.*
(Boulder, CO: Johnson Books, 2003).

Zwinger, Ann.
*Beyond the aspen grove.*
(New York: Random House, 1970).

## THE ALLURE OF WATER

**Books**

Allison, James.
*Water in the Garden: A complete guide to the design and installation of ponds, fountains, streams, and waterfalls.*
(Boston, Mass: Little Brown, 1991).

Nash, Helen.
*Low maintenance water gardens.*
(New York: Sterling, 1996).

Nash, Helen & Speichert, Greg.
*Water gardening in containers: small ponds, indoors & out.*
(New York: Sterling, 1996).

## THE ALLURE OF WATER (continued)

Slocum, Perry D., Robinson, Peter and Frances Perry.
*Water gardening: Water lilies and lotuses.*
(Portland, OR: Timber Press, 1996).

Speichert, Greg and Speichert, Sue.
*Encyclopedia of water garden plants.*
(Portland, OR: Timber Press, 2004).

**Articles**

Tomocik, Joe and Garisto, Leslie.
*Water gardening. (The American Garden Guides).*
(New York: Pantheon Books, 1996).

Tomocik, Joe.
"Make a big splash with a tiny water garden: Plunge into the world of aquatic plants by designing a minipond in a small container."
(*Fine Gardening* 56:56-61, July-August, 1997).

Tomocik, Joe, et al. (Spring 1997)
"Water gardening."
(*Mountain, Plain and Garden* 54:1:1-53, [entire issue], Spring 1997.)

**Web sites**

Colorado Water Gardening Society:
www.coloradowatergardens.org

International Waterlily and Water Gardening Society:
www.iwgs.org

## THE GARDENS UNDER GLASS

**Books**

Cunningham, Anne S.
*Crystal palaces, American garden conservatories.*
(New York: Princeton Architectural Press, 2000).

## THE GARDENS UNDER GLASS
**(continued)**

Llamas, Kirsten Albrecht.
*Tropical flowering plants: A guide to identification and cultivation.*
(Portland, OR: Timber Press, 2003).

Plotkin, Mark J.
*Tales of a shaman's apprentice: An ethnobotanist searches for new medicines in the amazon rainforest.*
(New York: Viking, 1993).

## VERSAILLES ON THE PLATTE
**Books**
Fox, Helen M. Andre
*Le Notre: Garden architect to kings.*
(New York: Crown Publishers, 1962).

Hazelhurst, F. Hamilton.
*Gardens of illusion: The genius of Andre Le Nostre.*
(Nashville, TN: Vanderbilt University Press, 1980).

MacDougall, Elisabeth B.
and F. Hamilton Hazlehurst, eds.
*The French formal garden.*
(Washington, DC: Dumbarton Oaks Trustees for Harvard University, 1974).

Morris, Alistair.
*Antiques from the garden.*
(Woodbridge, Suffolk: Garden Art Press, 1996).

Plumptre, George.
*Garden ornament: Five hundred years of history and practice.*
(London: Thames and Hudson, 1989).

Strong, Roy C.
*Creating formal gardens.*
(Boston: Little, Brown, 1989).

## VERSAILLES ON THE PLATTE
**(continued)**

Whalley, Robin and Anne Jennings.
*Knot gardens and parterres: A history of the knot garden and how to make one today.*
(London: Barn Elms in association with the Museum of Garden History, 1998).

## THE PUBLIC GARDEN AS SCIENCE
**Books**
Brower, Michael and Warren Leon.
*The consumer's guide to effective environmental choices: Practical advice from the union of concerned scientists.*
(New York: Three Rivers Press, 1999).

Diamond, Jared M.
*Guns, germs and steel: The fate of human societies.*
(New York: W.W. Norton, 1997).

Kingsolver, Barbara.
*Prodigal summer.*
(New York: Harper Collins Publishers, 2000).

Leopold, Aldo.
*A Sand County almanac.*
(New York: Oxford University Press, 2001).

Reaka-Kudla, Marjorie L., Wilson, Don. E.
and Edward O. Wilson, eds.
*Biodiversity II: Understanding and protecting our biological resources.*
(Washington, DC: Joseph Henry Press, 1997).

Slobodkin, Lawrence B.
*A citizen's guide to ecology.*
(New York: Oxford University Press, 2003).

Thoreau, Henry David.
*Walden.*
(New York: Oxford University Press, 1997).

# Appendix III: Index

*Abies lasiocarpa* 54
Acanthaceae 105
*Acantholimon* spp. 14
*Acer japonicum* 34
*Achillea* 'Moonshine' 5
*Achillea* 'Terracotta' 13
*Acorus calamus* 77
Adam's apple (*Tabernaemontana crassa*) 105
African daisy (*Arctotis*) 17
*Agastache barberi* 67, 69
*Agastache rupestris* 35, 69
*Agastache* spp. 40
*Agave* 13, 34, 39
*Agave asperrima* 11
*Agave parryi* 34, 38
*Agave parryi* ssp. *neomexicana* 35
*Aglaonema* 104
Agriculture 29
*Aiphanes aculeata* 102
Algae 77
Alkali sacaton (*Sporobolus airoides*) 143
All-America Selections 24
*Allium caeruleum* 19, 20
*Allium christophii* 38
*Allium* cvs. 40
*Allium flavum* 132
*Allium giganteum* 38
*Alocasia* 104
Alpine forget-me-not (*Eritrichium aretioides*) 54
Alpine paintbrush (*Castilleja puberula*) 58
Alpine phlox (*Phlox condensata*) 12
Alpine Rock Garden at Mount Goliath 23, 52, 57, 58
Alpine spring beauty (*Claytonia megarhiza*) 54
Alumroot (*Heuchera bracteata*) 58
Amaranth (*Amaranthus cruentus*) 6
American bistort (*Polygonum bistortoides*) 58
American lotus (*Nelumbo lutea*) 79
*Amorpha canescens* 29, 39
*Amorphophallus titanum* 104

*Ananas comosus* 97, 101
*Androsace chamaejasme* 48
Animal and Plant Health Inspection Service (APHIS) **See** U.S. Animal and Plant Health Inspection Service (APHIS)
Anna's Overlook 11, 24
Annuals 24, 32, 118
Ant feeder tree (*Cecropia peltata*) 96
Anthurium (*Anthurium* spp.) 104
Apache plume (*Fallugia paradoxa*) 42
Apocynaceae 105
*Aquilegia caerulea* 43
Araceae 104
Arapahoe County (CO) Soil Survey 1
*Arctotis* 17
*Areca vestiaria* 102
Arizona cypress (*Cupressus arizonica*) 39
Aroids 104
Aromatherapy 98
*Asclepias tuberosa* 66, 69
Aspen fleabane (*Erigeron speciosus*) 8
*Asplenium* spp. 101
*Aster fendleri* 68
*Astilbe* 36
Australian fan palm (*Licuala ramsayi*) 102
Austrian copper rose (*Rosa foetida* 'Bicolor') 1
Austrian yellow rose (*Rosa foetida*) 14
Autumn sage (*Salvia greggii*) 38, 127
Autumn sage (*Salvia greggii* 'Furman's Red') 131
Autumn sage (*Salvia greggii* Wild Thing™) 62, 69
Avens (*Geum* 'Borisii') 124
Avery Peak twinpod (*Physaria alpina*) 64, 66
Azaleas 34
*Azolla pinnata* 91

Ball, Ken 21
Balsa (*Ochroma pyramidale*) 98
Bamboo (*Bambusa* spp.) 14, 92, 98
Banana (*Musa* cvs.) 97

*Baptisia australis* 69
Barberry (*Berberis thunbergii* 'Aurea') 128
Barberry (*Berberis thunbergii* Crimson Pygmy 'Atropurpurea Nana') 128
Barr, Claude 47
Bayard, John 79
Beardtongue (*Penstemon grandiflorus*) 69
Beavertail pricklypear (*Opuntia basilaris*) 34
Beeplant (*Cleome serrulata*) 7
Beneficial insects 108
*Berberis thunbergii* 'Aurea' 128
*Berberis thunbergii* Crimson Pygmy 'Atropurpurea Nana' 128
*Berlandiera lyrata* 18
Berkeley Park, Denver, CO 78
Bibee, Ernest A. 109
Big Bugs 23
Biocontrols 137, 138, 141, 147
Biodiversity 8, 141, 145, 147
Biomes 8
BIOS, Inc. 109
Birds and Bees Garden 21
*Bismarckia nobilis* 102
Black pepper (*Piper nigrum*) 97
Black-eyed Susan (*Rudbeckia hirta*) 25
Blackfoot daisy (*Melampodium leucanthum*) 32
Blanket flower (*Gaillardia aristata*) 39, 47
Blue butterfly bush (*Clerodendrum ugandense*) 96
Blue Egyptian lotus (*Nymphaea caerulea*) 74, 83, 91
Blue globe onion (*Allium caeruleum*) 19, 20
Blue grama grass (*Bouteloua gracilis*) 42, 45
Blue oat grass (*Helictotrichon sempervirens*) 13
Blue-mist spirea (*Caryopteris* cvs.) 40
Bluestem joint fir (*Ephedra equisetina*) 40
Boettcher Foundation 109
Boettcher Tropical Conservatory 31, 41, 93, 94, 95, 96, 97, 98, 99, 101, 102, 104, 105, 107, 108, 109, 110
  history 109

152

renovation 110
Bonsai pines 25
Bosque 132, 138, 143
Botanic gardens ii, 92, 144
*Bothriochloa laguroides* ssp. *torreyana* 43
Boulder County, CO 26, 43
Boulders 48, 51, 57, 61, 65
*Bouteloua gracilis* 42, 45
Boxwood (*Buxus*) 128
Bracts 105
Brazilian red cloak (*Megaskepasma erythrochlamys*) 105
Bristlecone pine forest 48, 52, 54, 58
Bristlecone pines (*Pinus aristata*) 43, 46, 48, 49, 50, 52, 54, 56
*Bromeliaceae* 99, 100
Bromeliads 99, 100, 101, 110
*Bromus tectorum* 39, 138
Brooklyn (NY) Botanic Gardens 73
Brown-eyed Susan (*Rudbeckia triloba*) *inside front cover*
*Buchloe dactyloides* Legacy® and *B. dactyloides* 609 117, 121, 135
Buckwheat (*Eriogonum jamesii*) 41
Buckwheat (*Eriogonum* spp.) 37, 39, 41
Buffalo grass (*Buchloe dactyloides* Legacy® and *B. dactyloides* 609) 117, 121, 135
Bulbs 40, 122, 127, 131, 135
Butterfly milkweed (*Asclepias tuberosa*) 66, 69
Button snakewort (*Liatris spicata* 'Floristan Violett') 128
*Buxus* 128

Cacti 11, 13, 23, 24, 31, 35, 36, 39, 41, 65, 137, 141
 epiphytic 101
 foxtail (*Coryphantha missouriensis* 4)
 fruits 40
 tropical 106
Cactus and Succulent House 78
California fuschia (*Epilobium canum* ssp. *garrettii*) 65

California poppies (*Eschscholzia californica*) 37, 39
*Calliandra haematocephala* 96
*Callirhoe involucrata* 42
*Caltha leptosepala* 57
*Campanula rotundifolia* 43, 58
Canada geese 80
Canada thistle (*Cirsium arvense*) 138
*Canna* 'Australia' 83
*Canna* (*Canna* cvs.) 74, 77, 83
*Canna* 'Endeavour' 83
*Canna* 'Erebus,' 83
*Canna* 'Ra' 83
Cardinal's guard (*Pachystachys coccinea*) 105
*Carduus nutans* 137
*Carex morrowii* 'Ice Dance' 15
*Carica papaya* 97, 98
*Carludovica palmata* 98
Carnivorous plants 91, 107
*Caryopteris* cvs. 40
*Castilleja integra* 47
*Castilleja miniata* 58
*Castilleja occidentalis* 58
*Castilleja puberula* 58
*Castilleja rhexifolia* 58
Cattails (*Typha angustifolia, T. latifolia* and *T. laxmannii*) 77
Cattails (*Typha* spp.) 70, 77
*Celtis occidentalis* 84
*Cercocarpus ledifolius* 118, 119, 121, 128
*Cecropia peltata* 96
Centennial Gardens i, 11, 114, 117, 118, 121, 122, 127, 128, 132, 135
Center for Plant Conservation (St. Louis, MO) 145
*Chamaebatiaria millefolium* 40, 128
Champa tree (*Michelia champaca*) 98
Chappell, Dos 58
Chapungu 23
Chatfield *i*
Chatsworth, England 73, 77
Cheatgrass (*Bromus tectorum*) 39, 138

*Chilopsis linearis* 11
Chinese evergreen (*Aglaonema*) 104
Chinese juniper (*Juniperus chinensis* 'Blue Point') 124, 131
Chocolate 97, 113
Chocolate flower (*Berlandiera lyrata*) 18
Chocolate tree (*Theobroma cacao*) 97
Christmas cactus (*Schlumbergera* spp.) 101
*Chrysanthemum zawadskii* 'Clara Curtis' *inside front cover*
Cinquefoil (*Potentilla fruticosa*) 57
*Cirsium arvense* 138
*Cirsium ownbeyi* 136, 137, 145
Civitas, Denver, CO 118
Claret cup cactus (*Echinocereus triglochidiatus*) 34
*Claytonia megarhiza* 54
*Clematis columbiana* var. *tenuiloba* 43, 66
*Cleome serrulata* 7
*Clerodendrum ugandense* 96
 Climate 33
 region 8
 sister (to Colorado) 10, 14
Cloud forest 94, 106
Cloud Forest tree 24, 101, 106, 110, 111
*Coccoloba pubescens* 98
*Coelogyne speciosa* 99
*Coffea arabica* 97
*Coffea canephora* 97
Coffee 92, 97, 113
Colorado beardtongue (*Penstemon auriberbis*) 66
Colorado Plateau 7
Colorado Water Gardening Society 23, 77, 84, 88
Colorant 80
Comanche Grasslands, CO 61
Conifers 21, 24, 39, 42, 43, 46, 48, 49, 50, 52, 54, 56, 61, 118, 124, 127, 129, 131, 135, 147
Conservation ii, 91, 113, 137, 144
 ex-situ 145, 147
 things to consider 138

---

153

# Appendix III: Index

*Consolida ajacis* 14
Containers 24, 41, 62, 65, 69, 77, 79, 80, 82, 83, 88, 117, 118
Convention on International Trade in Endangered Species of Wild Fauna and Flora (CITES) 91
*Coreopsis verticillata* 'Moonbeam' 13
Corn (*Zea mays*) 6
Corn poppy (*Papaver rhoeas*) 20
*Coronilla varia* 143
Corpse flower (*Amorphophallus titanium*) 104
*Coryphantha missouriensis* 4
Cosmetics 98
*Cotoneaster apiculatus* 124, 134, 135
Cottonwood Border 22, 42
Cottonwoods (*Populus deltoides* ssp. *monilifera*) 26, 30, 42, 43, 138, 140, 142, 143
Crabapple (*Malus* 'Donald Wyman') 124, 131
Crabapple (*Malus ioensis* 'Prairiefire') 124
Cranberry cotoneaster (*Cotoneaster apiculatus*) 124, 134, 135
Crevice gardens 48, 58
Crevice, talus and scree plant community 52, 54
*Crocus* 40, 41, 122, 127, 135
   species 40
   spring 117, 132, 133
*Crocus chrysanthus* 132
*Crocus chrysanthus* 'Blue Pearl' 127
*Crocus vernus* 117, 132, 133
Cross Mountain Canyon, CO 136
*Crossandra infundibuliformis* 105
Crossroads 24
Crystal Palace 82
Cup plant (*Silphium perfoliatum*) 22
*Cupressus arizonica* 39
*Curcuma longa* 98
Curly-leaf mountain mahogany (*Cercocarpus ledifolius*) 118, 119, 121, 128
Cushion phlox (*Phlox pulvinata*) 58

Cutleaf daisy (*Erigeron compositus*) 57
Cutleaf sage (*Salvia jurisicii*) 40
Cutting Garden 21
*Cycas circinalis* 96
Cycads 96
*Cyperus alternifolius* 83
*Cyperus haspan* 83
*Cyperus papyrus* 83, 91

*Dasylirion* 13
Davis, Gary 109
Daylily (*Hemerocallis* 'Chicago Sunrise') 121
DeBoer, Sacco 21
*Delosperma cooperi* 17, 24, 132
*Delosperma floribundum* Starburst™ 127
*Delosperma* (Ice plant) 17, 18
*Delosperma* 'John Proffitt' 36, 127
*Delosperma* 'Kelaidis' Mesa Verde™ 17, 127
*Delosperma nubigenum* 17, 124, 132
*Delphinium* Summer Skies Group 120, 121
Demographics 145
*Dendrobium* 112
*Dendrobium lindleyi* 92
Denver 43, 48
Denver Botanic Gardens at Chatfield i
Denver Botanic Gardens Herbarium of Fungi 145
Denver Water 21, 33
Desert four o'clock (*Mirabilis multiflora* var. *glandulosa*) 42
Desert willow (*Chilopsis linearis*) 11
*Dianthus* 40
*Diascia* (Twinspur) 17
*Diascia integerrima* Coral Canyon™ 17
*Dieffenbachia* (Dumb cane) 104
*Dionaea muscipula* 91
*Dioon spinulosum* 96
Dolinski, Loddie 23
Dos Chappell Nature Center 48, 52, 53, 54, 55, 58
Drop Dead Red Border 21

*Drosera* spp. 91
Drought 7, 10, 11, 18, 24, 29, 35, 40, 41, 43, 101, 114, 117
Dry meadow 52, 54, 58
*Dryas octopetala* 66
Dryland Mesa 11, 13, 21, 23, 35, 41
Ducks 70, 71, 84
Dumb cane (*Dieffenbachia*) 104
Dust Bowl 29
Dwarf fishtail palm (*Gronophyllum pinangoides*) 102
Dwarf lavender (*Lavandula angustifolia* 'Hidcote' and *L. angustifolia* 'Munstead') 121
Dwarf papyrus (*Cyperus haspan*) 83
Dwarf upright spruce (*Picea glauca*) 118
*Dypsis decaryi* 96

East Indian lotus (*Nelumbo nucifera*) 74, 79
Easter cactus (*Rhipsalidopsis* spp.) 101
*Echinocereus reichenbachii* 31
*Echinocereus triglochidiatus* 34
Eckbo, Garrett 21
Ecological restoration 147
Ecosystems 62, 91, 92, 94, 96, 101, 105, 106, 113, 137, 138, 142, 143, 144, 145, 147
EDAW 21
El Pomar Waterway 23
*Eleagnus augustifolia* 2
Elephant's ear (*Alocasia*) 104
Elephant's heads (*Pedicularis groenlandica*) 57, 58
*Elymus trachycaulus* 142
Ember palm (*Areca vestiaria*) 102
Emperor Fountain, Chatsworth, England, 73
Encyclia 99
Engelmann spruce (*Picea engelmannii*) 54
*Ephedra equisetina* 40
*Epidendrum parkinsonianum* 99
*Epilobium canum* ssp. *garrettii* 65
*Epiphyllum* spp. 101
Epiphytes 24, 99, 101, 106, 111

*Eremurus* 40, 127
*Eremurus* 'Jeanne-Claire' 122
*Eremurus stenophyllus* 38
*Eremurus.* x *isabellinus* 'Pinokkio' and 'Cleopatra' 122
*Ericameria nauseosa* 6
*Ericameria* ssp. 27
*Erigeron compositus* 57
*Erigeron speciosus* 8
*Eriogonum jamesii* 41
*Eriogonum jamesii* var. *xanthum* 58, 59
*Eriogonum* spp. 37, 39, 41
*Eritrichium aretioides* 54
*Eschscholzia californica* 37, 39
Essential oils 98
*Eupatorium purpureum* inside front cover
*Euphorbia esula* 138
*Eustoma grandiflorum* 147
Evening primrose (*Oenothera* spp.) 47

*Fallugia paradoxa* 42
False indigo (*Baptisia australis*) 69
Feldspar 61
Fellfield 51, 52, 54, 58
Fendler's aster (*Aster fendleri*) 68
Fernbush (*Chamaebatiaria millefolium*) 40, 128
Ferns 101
Fertilizers 39, 41, 82
*Festuca idahoensis* 43
Firecracker flower (*Crossandra infundibuliformis*) 105
Floristics 8, 24
Fly Trap Feast display 88
Forbs 51, 57, 131, 142
Formal gardens 114, 115
  decorative accents 118
  elements of 117
  role of nature 121
  water features 115, 121
Fountains 74, 77, 114, 118

Foxtail barley (*Hordeum jubatum*) 32
Foxtail cactus (*Coryphantha missouriensis*) 4
Foxtail lily (*Eremurus* cvs.) 40, 127
Foxtail lily (*Eremurus* 'Jeanne-Claire', *E.* x *isabellinus* 'Pinokkio' and 'Cleopatra') 122
Foxtail lily (*Eremurus stenophyllus*) 38
Fragrance 131
Fragrance Garden 21
Freestone, Doris 88
*Fritillaria* 127
Front Range 2, 8, 10, 26, 28, 44, 48, 69
Front Range beardtongue (*Penstemon virens*) 57
Frost-heaving 39
Fungal spores 142
Fungi, Herbarium of, 145

*Gaillardia aristata* 39, 47
Garden Club of America 1
Garden Club of Denver 57, 58
Gates Montane Garden 11, 21
Gayfeather (*Liatris punctata*) 43, 47, 69
*Gazania* 17
*Gazania krebsiana* Tanager™ 36, 40
German statice (*Goniolimon tataricum*) 41
*Geum* 'Borisii' 124
Giant flowering onion (*Allium giganteum*) 38
Giant hyssop (*Agastache barberi*) 67, 69
Giant sacaton (*Sporobolus wrightii*) 39
*Glandularia peruviana* 127, 132
*Glaucium corniculatum* 10
Global warming 113
Golden elderberry (*Sambucus nigra* ssp. *canadensis* 'Aurea') 121
Golden pricklypear (*Opuntia aurea*) 35
Golden switch grass (*Panicum virgatum* 'Heavy Metal') 22, 124, 125
Goldenrod (*Solidago*) 39
*Goniolimon tataricum* 41
Granite 61, 66

Grasses *inside front cover*, 24, 26, 32, 36, 39, 43, 51, 57, 70, 124, 125, 128, 142
  in winter 41
Grasslands 7, 26, 44
Gray's peak, CO 52
Great American Desert 7, 26
Great Basin 7
Great Exhibition of 1851 82
Great Plains 7, 43, 47, 61, 62, 69
Great Sand Dunes, CO 47
*Gronophyllum pinangoides* 102
Groundsel (*Senecio vulgaris*) 39
Guava (*Psidium guajava*) 97

Hackberry (*Celtis occidentalis*) 84
Hailstorms 80, 82
Hammer, Lou 21
Hardscape 117, 118
Hardy canna (*Thalia dealbata*) 77
Hardy ice plant (*Delosperma cooperi*) 17, 24, 132
Hardy ice plant (*Delosperma nubigenum*) 17, 124, 132
Hardy sundaisy (*Osteospermum* spp.) 17
Harebells (*Campanula rotundifolia*) 43, 58
Harison's yellow rose (*Rosa* x *harisonii*) 1, 14
Hedges 114, 116, 118, 119, 121, 127, 128
Helen Fowler Library 77
*Helianthus annuus* 7, 26
*Heliconia orthotricha* 'Flash' 109
*Helictotrichon sempervirens* 13
*Hemerocallis* 'Chicago Sunrise' 121
Hen and chicks (*Sempervivum* spp.) 13
Henbit (*Lamium amplexicaule*) 39
Henrich, James 109
Herb Garden 24
Herbal medicines 145
Herbaria 145
Herbarium of Fungi, 145
Herbarium of Vascular Plants 145
Herbicides 141, 142, 147

155

# Appendix III: Index

*Hesperaloe* 13, 34, 38
*Hesperaloe parviflora* 34
*Huechera bracteata* 58
*Heuchera hallii* 66
*Hibiscus* 105
High Plains 7
Highveld 7
Honeysuckle (*Lonicera maackii*) 14
Honnen, Margaret E. "Marnie" 106
*Hordeum jubatum* 32
Horehound (*Marrubium rotundifolium*) 41
Horned poppy (*Glaucium corniculatum*) 10
Hornbein, Victor 109
Houseplants 101, 104
Hummingbirds 69
*Hyacinthus* 127
*Hymenoxys hoopesii* 46
Hypertufa 62, 69
Hyssop (*Agastache* spp.) 40

Ice plants 17, 18, 24, 36, 124, 132
Idaho fescue (*Festuca idahoensis*) 43
*Iguanura spectabilis* 102
Indian paintbrush (*Castilleja integra*) 47
Indian paintbrush (*Castilleja miniata*) 58
Indian Peaks, CO 26
Indian saffron (*Curcuma longa*) 98
Integrated Pest Management (IPM) 91, 108
International Waterlily and Water Gardening Society 88
Iris 14, 127
  bearded 39
*Iris lactea* iii
*Iris pallida* 'Variegata' 123
*Iris reticulata* 38, 40

Jacob's ladder (*Polemonium pulcherrimum* ssp. *delicatum*) 58
James' buckwheat (*Eriogonum jamesii* var. *xanthum*) 58, 59
Japanese Garden 25, 31
Japanese maple (*Acer japonicum*) 34
Japanese sedge (*Carex morrowii* 'Ice Dance') 15
*Jewels of the Plains* 47
Joe Pye weed (*Eupatorium purpureum*) inside front cover
Joey palm (*Johannesteijsmannia altifrons*) 102, 103
*Johannesteijsmannia altifrons* 102, 103
June's PlantAsia 11, 14, 15, 23, 24
Junipers (*Juniperus* spp.) 24, 39, 61, 124, 127, 131, 135
*Juniperus chinensis* 'Blue Point' 124, 131
*Juniperus scopulorum* 'Wichita Blue' 124, 127, 129, 131
*Juniperus squamata* 'Blue Star' 131

Karoo 7, 17
Kathryn Kalmbach Herbarium of Vascular Plants 145
Kawahara, Kai 21
Kawana, Koichi 21
Kelaidis, Gwen 1
Kelly, George 1, 2
*Kerriodoxa elegans* 102
Kew Gardens, London, England 73
King Louis XIV 114, 132
Kitchen Garden 23
*Kniphofia* 'Alcazar' 16
*Kniphofia* 'Cobra' 25
*Kniphofia* 'Shining Sceptre' 5
*Kniphofia uvaria* 'Royal Castle Hybrids' 16
Knot gardens 24
Kondo, Ebi 23
Krummholz 52, 54, 58
Kudzu vine 2

Lace hedgehog cactus (*Echinocereus reichenbachii*) 31
Lamb's ear (*Stachys*) 37
*Lamium amplexicaule* 39
Land management practices 137, 138, 141
Landon, Ken 83, 84
Landscape architects 21
Larkspur (*Consolida ajacis*) 14
Latour-Marliac, Joseph Bory 84
Laura Smith Porter Plains Garden 24, 32, 33, 35, 38, 41, 42
*Lavandula angustifolia* 'Hidcote' 121, 128
*Lavandula angustifolia* 'Munstead' 121, 128
Lavender 38
Lavender (*Lavandula angustifolia* 'Hidcote') 121, 128
Lavender (*Lavandula angustifolia* 'Munstead') 121, 128
Lavender cotton (*Santolina chamaecyparissus*) 121, 128
Lavender cotton (*Santolina rosmarinifolia*) 121, 128, 132
Le Nôtre, André 73, 114
Lead plant (*Amorpha canescens*) 29, 39
Leafy spurge (*Euphorbia esula*) 138
*Lepidium latifolium* 138
*Lesquerella ovalifolia* ssp. *ovalifolia* 66
*Lewisia cotyledon* title page
*Leymus triticoides* 143
*Liatris punctata* 43, 47, 69
*Liatris spicata* 'Floristan Violett' 128
Lichens 99
*Licuala ramsayi* 102
Lilacs 14
Lilies 13
Lilyturf (*Liriope muscari*) 15
Limber pine (*Pinus flexilis*) 61
*Limonium* spp. 39
Linden (*Tilia cordata* Greenspire® 'PNI 6025') 118, 121, 127, 131
Lindgren, Dale 13
Lindley, John 77
*Liriope muscari* 15
Little bluestem (*Schizachyrium scoparium*) 43
Little pickles (*Othonna capensis*) 17
Littleleaf alumroot (*Heuchera hallii*) 66
Lizard tail palm (*Iguanura spectabilis*) 102

Lollipop plant (*Pachystachys lutea*) 105
Long, Stephen 7
Longstock Gardens, England 73
Longwood Gardens, PA 73
*Lonicera maackii* 14
Loosestrife (*Lythrum salicaria*) 91
Los Lunas Plant Materials Center, NM 13
Lotus 74, 76
  cultivation 79
  *Nelumbo* 74
  *Nelumbo* cvs. 24, 83, 84
  *Nelumbo* 'Jade Bowl' 79
  *Nelumbo lutea* 79
  *Nelumbo nucifera* 74, 79
  *Nelumbo nucifera* 'Mrs. Perry D. Slocum' 79, 81
  *Nelumbo* 'Ohga Hasu' 80
  *Nelumbo* 'Perry's Giant Sunburst' 79
  overwintering 80
  seed pod 74
  viable seed 80
Lotusland, Santa Barbara, CA 73
*Lythrum salicaria* 91

M. Walter Pesman trail 48, 52, 57, 58
*Machaeranthera bigelovii* 6
*Machaeranthera* spp. 34
*Mahonia repens* 43
Malanga (*Xanthosoma*) 104
*Malus* 'Donald Wyman' 124, 131
*Malus ioensis* 'Prairiefire' 131
Malvaceae 105
Marginals 70, 77, 83
Marnie's Pavilion 101, 106, 108, 110
*Marrubium* 37
*Marrubium rotundifolium* 41
Marsh marigold (*Caltha leptosepala*) 57
Maslin, Paul 1
May Bonfils-Stanton Memorial Rose Garden 23
McLane, Bruce and Brad 84

Medicinal plants 98
Mediterranean 24, 34
Mediterranean climate 4, 44
Mediterranean plants 34
Mediterranean silver sage (*Salvia argentea*) 38
*Megaskepasma erythrochlamys* 105
*Melampodium leucanthum* 32
*Mentzelia decapetala* 35
Mesa de Maya, CO 61
Mexican cycad (*Dioon spinulosum*) 96
Mexican feather grass (*Nassella tenuissima*) 39
*Michelia champaca* 98
Microclimates 34, 38, 39
Midge larvae 82
Mile High Border 5, 23, 25
*Minuartia obtusiloba* 58
*Mirabilis multiflora* var. *glandulosa* 42
Mirgon, John and Mary 88
*Miscanthus sinensis* 'Zebrinus' *inside front cover*
Missouri Botanical Garden 73, 82
Mojave sage (*Salvia pachyphylla*) 9, 35
Monet Deck Café 84
Monet Garden 23
Monet Garden's horseshoe pool 70, 72, 84
Monet Water Garden 89
Monet's water gardens 84
*Montezuma speciosissima* 105
Moritz, Chris 21
Mosquito Range Trough 66
Moss campion (*Silene acaulis*) 54, 58
Mosses 99
Mount Evans, CO 52, 61
Mount Evans Trough 12
Mount Goliath, CO i, 48, 52, 54, 57, 58
Mount of the Holy Cross, CO 52
Mountain avens (*Dryas octopetala*) 66
Mountain-grape (*Coccoloba pubescens*) 98
Mountain mahogany (*Cercocarpus ledifolius*) 118, 119, 121, 128

Mulches 33, 57, 140
  gravel 39, 43
  gravel vs. organic 39
  pea gravel 69
  rock 69, 118
Mullein (*Verbascum* spp.) 39
*Musa* cvs. 97
*Muscari* spp. 127
Musk thistle (*Carduus nutans*) 137

*Nassella tenuissima* 39
National Center for Genetics Resources Preservation, Fort Collins, CO 145
National parks 113
Native plants 9, 13, 18, 29, 33, 34, 35, 36, 39, 41, 57, 114, 117, 137, 138, 142, 143, 145
*Nelumbo* 74
*Nelumbo* cvs. 24, 83, 84
*Nelumbo* 'Jade Bowl' 79
*Nelumbo lutea* 79
*Nelumbo nucifera* 74, 79
*Nelumbo nucifera* 'Mrs. Perry D. Slocum' 79, 81
*Nelumbo* 'Ohga Hasu' 80
*Nelumbo* 'Perry's Giant Sunburst' 79
Nelumbonaceae 74
*Nepenthes* 106, 107
*Nepenthes alata* 107
Netted iris (*Iris reticulata*) 38, 40
New Mexico agave (*Agave parryi* ssp. *neomexicana*) 35
New Mexico figwort (*Scrophularia macrantha*) 13, 69
*Nolina microcarpa* 35
Noxious weeds 91, 137, 138
*Nuphar* 77
*Nuphar lutea* 91
Nutt, Patrick 73, 82, 84
*Nymphaea* 70, 74, 76, 77, 79, 81, 83, 84
*Nymphaea* 'Albert Greenberg' 84
*Nymphaea* 'Amabilis' 84
*Nymphaea caerulea* 74, 83, 91

# Appendix III: Index

*Nymphaea capensis* 83
*Nymphaea* 'Denver's Delight' 78
*Nymphaea* 'Devonshire' 91
*Nymphaea* 'Escarboucle' 84
*Nymphaea gracilis* 83
*Nymphaea* 'Indiana' 84, 90
*Nymphaea* 'Lindsey Woods' 73
*Nymphaea lotus* 83
*Nymphaea* 'Mary' 80
*Nymphaea mexicana* 84
*Nymphaea odorata* 84
*Nymphaea* 'Pygmaea Helvola' 84
*Nymphaea* 'Rhonda Kay' 83
*Nymphaea* 'star waterlilies' 83
*Nymphaea tetragona* 84
*Nymphaea* 'Virginalis' 84
*Nymphaeaceae* 77

O'Fallon Perennial Border 21, 24
*Oenothera* spp. 47
Old man of the mountain (*Tetraneuris grandiflora*) 12, 53, 54
*Oncidium* 99
*Ochroma pyramidale* 98
*Opuntia aurea* 35
*Opuntia basilaris* 34
*Opuntia phaeacantha* var. *major* 41
*Opuntia* spp. 11, 137
Orchid cactus (*Epiphyllum* spp.) 101
*Orchidaceae* 99
Orchids 92, 97, 99, 101, 110, 112
Oregon grape holly (*Mahonia repens*) 43
Ornamental onion (*Allium* cvs.) 40
Ornamental onion (*Allium flavum*) 132
*Osteospermum* 17
*Othonna capensis* 17
Ownbey's thistle (*Cirsium ownbeyi*) 136, 137, 145

*Pachystachys coccinea* 105
*Pachystachys lutea* 105
Paintbrush (*Castilleja occidentalis*) 58
Paintbrush (*Castilleja rhexifolia*) 58
Palm seed oil 98
Palms 96, 102, 103
Pampas 7
Panama hat plant (*Carludovica palmata*) 98
Panama hats 98
*Panicum virgatum* 'Heavy Metal' 22, 124, 125
Pansies (*Viola* x *wittrockiana* cvs.) 118, 122, 124, 127
*Papaver rhoeas* 20
Papaya (*Carica papaya*) 97, 98
Paperflower (*Psilostrophe tagetina*) 9
Papyrus (*Cyperus haspan*) 83
Papyrus (*Cyperus papyrus*) 83, 91
Parasites 99
*Paronychia pulvinata* 51, 54
Parrot beak flower (*Heliconia orthotricha* 'Flash') 109
Parry's agave (*Agave parryi*) 34, 38
Parterre 117, 118, 121, 122, 127, 128, 131
*Pascopyrum smithii* 34, 143
Patchouli (*Pogostemon cablin*) 98
Pawnee Buttes, CO 61
Paxton, Joseph 73
Peace, Tom 21
*Pedicularis groenlandica* 57, 58
Pedocals 8
Peduncles 83
*Pennisetum alopecuroides* 'Hameln' 128
Penstemon 13, 18, 43
*Penstemon auriberbis* 66
*Penstemon barbatus* 'Prairie Dusk' 38
*Penstemon cobaea* x *P. triflorus* 39
*Penstemon digitalis* 'Husker Red' 13
*Penstemon grandiflorus* 69
*Penstemon pinifolius* 124
*Penstemon pinifolius* 'Mersea Yellow' 124
*Penstemon strictus* 33, 46, 121
*Penstemon strictus* 'Bandera' 13

*Penstemon versicolor* 66
*Penstemon virens* 57
*Penstemon* x *mexicali* Red Rocks™ 18
Peonies 14, 32
Pepperweed (*Lepidium latifolium*) 138
*Perovskia atriplicifolia* inside front cover, 40, 132
Perry's Giant Sunburst lotus (*Nelumbo* 'Perry's Giant Sunburst') 79
Persian onion (*Allium christophii*) 38
Peruvian verbena (*Glandularia peruviana*) 127, 132
Pesman, M. Walter 57
Petioles 102
*Phacelia sericea* 55, 57
*Philodendron* 104
Phipps, Gerald H. 109
*Phlox condensata* 12
*Phlox pulvinata* 58
*Phyllostachys aureosulcata* 14
*Phyllostachys glauca* 14
*Phyllostachys nuda* 14
*Physaria alpina* 64, 66
*Picea engelmannii* 54
*Picea glauca* 118
Pikes Peak, CO 26, 61, 66
Piña cloth 98
Pincushion flower (*Scabiosa* 'Butterfly Blue') 124
Pineapple (*Ananas comosus*) 97, 101
Pineleaf penstemon (*Penstemon pinifolius*) 124
Pink creeping thyme (*Thymus serpyllum* 'Pink Chintz') 38
Piñon pines (*Pinus edulis*) 61
*Pinus aristata* 43, 46, 48, 49, 50, 52, 56
*Pinus edulis* 61
*Pinus flexilis* 61
*Pinus ponderosa* 21, 43, 147
Pioneers 1, 14, 28, 29
*Piper nigrum* 97
Pitcher plant (*Nepenthes alata*) 107
Pitcher plant (*Sarracenia oreophila*) 91

Pitcher plant (*Sarracenia rubra*) 91
Pitcher plant (*Sarracenia rubra* ssp. *alabamensis*) 91
Pitcher plant (*Sarracenia rubra* ssp. *jonesii*) 91
Pitcher plants 106, 107
Plains cottonwood (*Populus deltoides* ssp. *monilifera*) 26, 30, 42, 43, 138, 140, 143
Plains Garden 11, 21
Plant Select 1, 18, 35
Platte River, CO 26
*Platycerium bifurcatum* 101
*Plumeria* 112
*Pogostemon cablin* 98
*Polemonium pulcherrimum* ssp. *delicatum* 58
*Polemonium viscosum* 54, 58
Pollinators 127, 131, 135, 143
*Polygonum bistortoides* 58
Ponderosa Border 43
Ponderosa pines (*Pinus ponderosa*) 21, 43, 147
Poppies 39
Population models 145
*Populus deltoides* ssp. *monilifera* 26, 30, 42, 43, 138, 140, 142, 143
Portland cement 62, 65, 69
*Potentilla fruticosa* 57
Prairie 7, 8, 24, 26, 28, 32, 42, 43, 44, 47, 48
Prairie aster (*Machaeranthera bigelovii*) 6
Prairie coneflower (*Ratibida columnifera*) 29
Prairie cordgrass (*Spartina pectinata*) 77, 84
Prairie gentian (*Eustoma grandiflorum*) 147
Prairie winecups (*Callirhoe involucrata*) 42
Prairie zinnia (*Zinnia grandiflora*) 11
Precipitation rates 10
Prescribed burns 147
Preserves 113
Prickly pear (*Opuntia phaeacantha* var. *major*) 41
Prickly pear (*Opuntia* spp.) 11
Prickly spikethrifts (*Acantholimon* spp.) 14
Pring, Dr. George H. 73

Proctor, Rob 21, 122
Pruning 108, 117
*Prunus pumila* var. *besseyi* Pawnee Buttes™ 13
*Psidium guajava* 97
*Psilostrophe tagetina* 9
Puerto Rico hibiscus (*Montezuma speciosissima*) 105
Puna 7
Purple crownvetch (*Coronilla varia*) 143
Purple fringe (*Phacelia sericea*) 55, 57
Purple gayfeather (*Liatris punctata*) 43, 47, 69
Purple ice plant (*Delosperma cooperi*) 17, 24, 132

Queen sago (*Cycas circinalis*) 96

Rabbit Mountain Open Space, CO 146
Rabbitbrush (*Ericameria nauseosa*) 6
Rabbitbrush (*Ericameria* ssp.) 27
Rainfall 44
Rainforest 94, 113
*Ratibida columnifera* 29
Rattan 98
Rausch, Geoffey 21
Re-vegetation 142
Recycling 113
Red powderpuff (*Calliandra haematocephala*) 96
Red Rocks™ penstemon (*Penstemon* x *mexicali* Red Rocks™) 18
Red-flower yucca (*Hesperaloe parviflora*) 34
Reflection pool 75, 83, 85
Reflection statue 83
Reis, Jane Silverstein 21
*Rhaphidophora* (Shingle plant) 104
*Rhinocyllus conicus* 137
*Rhipsalidopsis* spp. 101
*Rhododendron* spp. 36, 106
Rock Alpine Garden 20, 21, 24, 31, 60
Rock clematis (*Clematis columbiana* var. *tenuiloba*) 43, 66
Rock jasmine (*Androsace chamaejasme*) 48

Rock soapwort (*Saponaria ocymoides* 'Alba') 61
Rocks 48, 51, 57, 61
  adding to home garden 58
  mulches 69, 118
Rocky Mountain Arsenal National Wildlife Refuge, CO 147
Rocky Mountain columbine (*Aquilegia caerulea*) 43
Rocky Mountain juniper (*Juniperus scopulorum* 'Wichita Blue') 124, 127, 129, 131
Rocky Mountain nailwort (*Paronychia pulvinata*) 51, 54
Rocky Mountain National Park, CO 9
Rocky Mountain penstemon (*Penstemon strictus*) 33, 46, 121
Rocky Mountain zinnia (*Zinnia grandiflora*) 11, 13, 129, 135
Rollinger, Al 1
Romantic Gardens 21, 24, 78
Romantic Gardens pool 79, 80, 81
*Rosa foetida* 14
*Rosa foetida* 'Bicolor' 1
*Rosa* 'Golden Unicorn' 130, 131
*Rosa* 'Linda Campbell' 116, 121
*Rosa* x *harisonii* 1, 14
Rosaceae 128
Rose Garden 21
Rose Garden pool 83
Rough agave (*Agave asperrima*) 11
Roundleaf bladderpod (*Lesquerella ovalifolia* ssp. *ovalifolia*) 66
Royal Botanic Gardens, Edinburgh, Scotland 62
Royal Horticultural Society Gardens, England 73
*Rudbeckia hirta* 25
*Rudbeckia triloba* inside front cover
Ruffle palm (*Aiphanes aculeata*) 102
Rushes 70
Russian olive (*Eleagnus augustifolia*) 2
Russian sage (*Perovskia atriplicifolia*) inside front cover,

# Appendix III: Index

40, 132

Sacahuista (*Nolina microcarpa*) 35
Sacred Earth 11
Sacred Earth pool 83
*Salacca magnifica* 102
Salak palm (*Salacca magnifica*) 102
Saltcedar **See** *Tamarix* spp.
*Salvia* 37, 38
*Salvia argentea* 38, 41
*Salvia greggii* 38, 127
*Salvia greggii* 'Furman's Red' 131
*Salvia greggii* Wild Thing™ 62, 69
*Salvia jurisicii* 40
*Salvinia molesta* 91
*Salvia pachyphylla* 9, 35
*Sambucus nigra* ssp. *canadensis* 'Aurea' 121
San Luis Valley, CO 27
Sandstone 118
*Santolina chamaecyparissus* 121, 128
*Santolina rosmarinifolia* 121, 128, 132
*Saponaria ocymoides* 'Alba' 61
*Sarracenia oreophila* 91
*Sarracenia rubra* 91
*Sarracenia rubra* ssp. *alabamensis* 91
*Sarracenia rubra* ssp. *jonesii* 91
Savanna 7
*Scabiosa* 'Butterfly Blue' 124
Scarlet bugler (*Penstemon barbatus* 'Prairie Dusk') 38
Schaal, Herb 21
*Schizachyrium scoparium* 43
Schlessman Plaza 21
*Schlumbergera* spp. 101
Scripture Garden 21
*Scrophularia macrantha* 13, 69
Sculptures 74, 83, 87, 114
Sea lavender (*Limonium* spp.) 39
Sedges 15, 57, 58
Seed bank 39, 145, 147

*Sempervivum* spp. 13
*Senecio vulgaris* 39
Sensory Garden 21
Shady Lane 23
Shingle plant 104
Shofu-en 21, 25
*Silene acaulis* 54, 58
*Silphium perfoliatum* 22
Silver beardgrass (*Bothriochloa laguroides* ssp. *torreyana*) 43
Silver sage (*Salvia argentea*) 38, 41
Sky pilot (*Polemonium viscosum*) 54, 58
Slocum, Perry D. 79, 84
Smith, Mrs. Walter R. 101
Snowbed communities 52
Soils 33, 65
    formation 51
    nutrient content 48
    organic 34, 107
    prairie 8
    preparation 33
    tropical 107, 108, 113
    tundra 51
*Solidago* 39
Sotol (*Dasylirion*) 13
South African border 16
South African Plaza 17, 21, 24
Southwestern willow flycatcher 143
Spanish moss (*Tillandsia usneoides*) 98, 101
*Spartina pectinata* 77, 84
*Spathiphyllum* 104
Spatterdock (*Nuphar lutea*) 91
Spatterdocks (*Nuphar*) 77
*Sporobolus airoides* 143
*Sporobolus wrightii* 39
Spring crocus (*Crocus vernus*) 117, 132, 133
Springer Ogden, Lauren 13, 21
*Stachys* 37
Staghorn fern (*Platycerium bifurcatum*) 101

Stapeley Water Gardens, England 73
Star gentian (*Swertia perennis*) 57
Stemless four-nerve daisy (*Tetraneuris acaulis* var. *acaulis*) 54
Stemmadenia (*Stemmadenia litoralis*) 105
Steppe 7, 8, 10, 14, 17, 24, 44, 88, 132
Strawn, Dr. Kirk 84
Styler, Trey and Nancy 82
Subalpine fir (*Abies lasiocarpa*) 54
Succulents 13, 23, 24
Summit Lake, CO 52
Sundew (*Drosera* spp.) 91
Sunflower (*Helianthus annuus*) 7, 26
Sunset hyssop (*Agastache rupestris*) 35, 69
Sustainability ii, 28, 29, 113, 138, 144
Swanson, Frank 83
Sweet flag (*Acorus calamus*) 77
*Swertia perennis* 57
Swift, Harry 1
Switch grass (*Panicum virgatum* 'Heavy Metal') 22, 124, 125

*Tabebuia* ssp. 98
*Tabernaemontana crassa* 105
Tamarisk (*Tamarix* spp.) 2, 138, 139, 140, 141, 142, 143, 147
Tansy aster (*Machaeranthera* spp.) 34
Taro (*Xanthosoma*) 104
Tatroe, Marcia 23
Teacup lotus (*Nelumbo* 'Jade Bowl') 79
Teak 98
Ten-petal blazing star (*Mentzelia decapetala*) 35
*Tetraneuris acaulis* var. *acaulis* 54
*Tetraneuris grandiflora* 12, 53, 54
*Thalia dealbata* 77
*Theobroma cacao* 97
Thompson's yucca (*Yucca thompsoniana*) 31, 38
Thurston, William and Mickie 99
Thymes 38

*Thymus serpyllum* 'Pink Chintz' 38
Tickseed (*Coreopsis verticillata* 'Moonbeam') 13
*Tilia cordata* Greenspire® 'PNI 6025' 118, 121, 127, 131
*Tillandsia usneoides* 98, 101
Torch lily (*Kniphofia* 'Alcazar') 16
Torch lily (*Kniphofia* 'Cobra') 25
Torch lily (*Kniphofia* 'Shining Sceptre') 5
Torch lily (*Kniphofia uvaria* 'Royal Castle Hybrids') 16
Torrey's peak, CO 52
Treeline 48, 54, 66
Triangle palm (*Dypsis decaryi*) 96
Trilliums 34
Tropical cacti 106
Tropical plants 92, 96, 98
  maintenance 107, 108
  pruning 108
Tropical rainforest 96,
  destruction of 113
  lowland 24, 94, 99
  products from 97
  upland 94
Troughs 62, 63, 66
  making 65, 69
*Tulipa* 'Golden Apeldoorn' 127
*Tulipa linifolia* 127
*Tulipa* 'Madame Lefeber' 126
Tulips 14, 122, 127
  species 40
Tundra 24, 48, 51, 54, 57, 69
Turkish veronica (*Veronica liwanensis*) 14, 124
Twinflower sandwort (*Minuartia obtusiloba*) 58
Twinspur (*Diascia*) 17
*Typha angustifolia* 77
*Typha latifolia* 77
*Typha laxmannii* 77
*Typha* spp. 70, 77

U.S. Animal and Plant Health Inspection Service (APHIS) 91
U.S. Forest Service 57, 58
Ultraviolet light 48, 51
Umbrella plant (*Cyperus alternifolius*) 83
University of Nebraska North Platte Experiment Station 13

*Vanda* Tokyo Blue 'Sapphire' 101
Vanilla 97
Vanilla orchid (*Vanilla planifolia*) 97
Venus flytraps (*Dionaea muscipula*) 91
*Verbascum* spp. 39
*Veronica liwanensis* 14, 124
Versailles Gardens 73, 114, 128, 132
*Victoria amazonica* 73, 77, 82
Victoria Conservancy 82
*Victoria cruziana* 82, 84
*Victoria* 'Longwood Hybrid' 82, 84
Victoria pool 82, 88
Victoria waterlilies 24, 73, 77, 83, 84
  growing 82
Victorian Secret Garden 23
Villa d'Este, Italy 73
*Viola x wittrockiana* cvs. 118, 122, 124, 127, 131
Vireya rhododendrons (*Rhododendron laetum* and *Rhododendron zoelleri*) 106
Volunteers for Outdoor Colorado 57, 58

Water conservation 32, 34, 135
Water consumption 10, 28, 29, 39, 40, 41
Water gardens 23, 70, 73, 74, 91
  Asian 73
  container 88
  creating 77
  European 73
  history 73
Water tables 10
Water-Smart Garden 11, 13, 21, 31, 36, 37, 38, 40

  care 38, 39
Water-Smart Gardening i, 11, 13, 25
*Waterlily*
  *Nymphaea* 70, 74, 76, 77, 79, 81, 83, 84
  *Nymphaea* 'Amabilis' 84
  *Nymphaea caerulea* 74, 83, 91
  *Nymphaea capensis* 83
  *Nymphaea* 'Denver's Delight' 78
  *Nymphaea* 'Devonshire' 91
  *Nymphaea* 'Escarboucle' 84
  *Nymphaea gracilis* 83
  *Nymphaea* 'Indiana' 84, 90
  *Nymphaea* 'Lindsey Woods' 73
  *Nymphaea lotus* 83
  *Nymphaea* 'Mary' 80
  *Nymphaea mexicana* 84
  *Nymphaea odorata* 84
  *Nymphaea* 'Pygmaea Helvola' 84
  *Nymphaea* 'Rhonda Kay' 83
  *Nymphaea* 'star waterlilies' 83
  *Nymphaea tetragona* 84
  *Nymphaea* 'Virginalis' 84
Waterways 23, 78
  black-colored water 80
Webb, Mayor Wellington 114
Weeds 34, 39, 141
  invasive 141, 147
  noxious 91, 137, 138
Weevil (*Rhinocyllus conicus*) 137
Weinstein, Gayle 21, 32
Western Panoramas 11, 22, 23, 24, 43
Western sneezeweed (*Hymenoxys hoopesii*) 46
Western wheatgrass (*Pascopyrum smithii*) 34, 143
Wet meadow 52, 58
Wheatgrass (*Elymus trachycaulus*) 142
White elephant palm (*Kerriodoxa elegans*) 102
White, Edward D. 109
Whitewood (*Tabebuia* ssp.) 98
Wild rye (*Leymus triticoides*) 143

# Appendix III: Index

Wildflower Treasures 11, 12, 21, 23, 62, 63, 65, 66
Willow trees 138, 143
Winch, Charles 84
Woodland Mosaic 21

*Xanthosoma* 104
Xeriscape 10, 13, 33, 36, 122
  design 33
Xeriscape Demonstration Garden 33, 35, 38

Yampa River 136
Yarrow (*Achillea* 'Moonshine') 5
Yarrow (*Achillea* 'Terracotta') 13
Yucca 13, 31, 34, 37, 38
*Yucca thompsoniana* 31, 38
Yuccarama 13

*Zea mays* 6
*Zinnia grandiflora* 11, 13, 129, 135
Zvolanek, Zdenek 57

# Denver Botanic Gardens

- Tea House
- Cutting Garden
- Japanese Garden
- Water Garden
- Monet Garden
- Victorian Secret Garden
- Shady Lane
- Oak Grove
- Wildflower Treasures
- Plains Garden
- AAS Garden
- Kitchen Garden
- Montane Garden
- Dryland Mesa
- Sacred Earth
- Rose Garden
- Succulent House
- South African Plaza
- Lilac Garden
- PlantAsia
- Ornamental Grasses
- Rock Alpine Garden
- Dwarf Conifer Berm
- Birds and Bees Walk
- Woodland Mosaic

# 11th Avenue

- Community Gardens
- Morrison Center
- Sensory Garden
- Gates Hall
- Helen Fowler Library
- Tropical Conservatory
- Cloud Forest Tree
- Mitchell Hall
- Gift Shop
- Community Gardens
- Water-Smart Garden
- Yuccarama
- Front Gate
- Cottonwood Border
- Ponderosa Border
- Children's Secret Path
- Perennial Walk
- Mile High Garden
- Bristlecone Border
- El Pomar Waterway
- Anna's Overlook
- Romantic Gardens
- York Street
- Scripture Garden
- Herb Garden

Map not to scale

Denver Botanic Gardens

## Gardening with Altitude:
*Cultivating a New Western Style*

# Appendix IV: Order Form

Name: _____

Address: _____

City, State, Zip:_____/_____/_____

Phone:_____ E-mail: _____

Gardens member number (please include expiration date):_____ Exp. date: _____

Please ship me ____ copies of Gardening with Altitude

Number of copies: _____

Price per copy: $29.95

Price with 10% Gardens Membership discount: $26.96

(membership info must be completed above)

Shipping: $4.50

Subtotal: _____

Tax (see box below): _____

TOTAL: _____

Check enclosed:_____ Credit card number:_____ Expiration date: _____

**Sales tax:**
Denver residents who are Gardens members - $2.05 per book
Denver residents who are not Gardens members - $2.28 per book
Colorado residents (living outside Denver) who are Gardens members - $1.11 per book
Colorado residents (living outside Denver) who are not Gardens members - $1.23 per book

**Fax your completed form with payment to 720-865-3731,
or mail it to the Helen Fowler Library, Denver Botanic Gardens, 909 York St., Denver, CO 80206.**